"Busy Christians in an iPhone age can loo[l] and we are the smartphone. We 'plug i[n] live on that energy until our spiritual batt[eries run dry—then we build up again at] time, conference, or retreat. But this is not a metaphor the Bible invites us to use when it speaks of our union in Christ. He is the vine; we are the branches. In her newest and perhaps most important work, my friend Elyse Fitzpatrick describes this beautiful union we have with our Savior and the joys of drawing from the Vine. I highly recommend this exceptional book!"
**Joni Eareckson Tada,** Founder and CEO, Joni and Friends International Disability Center

"*Found in Him* reveals the God-designed remedy for our impoverished hearts—the work of Christ for, in, and through us. While many heavy-laden, conscience-stricken believers struggle to bear up under the weight of their spiritual 'to-do' lists, Elyse awakens our hearts and minds to what Jesus has already done and calls us to find rest in him."
**Nancy DeMoss Wolgemuth,** author; Radio Host, *Revive Our Hearts*

"Fasten your seatbelt and get ready for a theological thrill ride. I'm not talking about spiritual entertainment—you best look elsewhere for that. But if you are looking to understand one of the most profound and moving mysteries of the Christian life—as Elyse puts it, 'the soul-consoling, heart-transforming, zeal-engendering' of Christ's incarnation and union with us—well, you've found the book you absolutely need to read."
**Mark Galli,** Editor in Chief, *Christianity Today*

"If Elyse Fitzpatrick is right, the Bible (finally) is not about us at all! It is about the God who has acted to save those who *don't* and *can't* 'become better,' and that Christianity is *not* (finally) about 'morals' at all. The Bible's story is a story about God's love for *immorals* like you and me. It is about Christ, who he is and what he did *for* us—once and for all and at a particular time and place in normal history."
**Rod Rosenbladt,** Former Professor of Theology, Concordia University, Irvine, California

"When the great theologian John Murray famously wrote, 'Union with Christ is really the central truth of the whole doctrine of salvation,' I wonder how I could have missed the point for so many years. Yet, as I simply consider the focus of Christ and the apostles on being 'in him,' I have grown to recognize the wisdom of Murray's words and now, with Elyse Fitzpatrick's book, I also cherish the dearness of them. She writes of the deep truths of our union with God, freshly unfolding biblical passages that describe his incarnation, and she writes with sensitivity of the significance of the continuing intimacy we have with the Creator who walked among us. Here is the infinite made intimate to strengthen our hearts."
**Bryan Chapell,** President Emeritus, Covenant Theological Seminary

"Over the years, I have been challenged by Elyse's profound and practical approach to biblical issues that concern women. Last year when I heard her share a snippet of her writing on the incarnation, I was hungry for more—and I wasn't disappointed! Pondering the incarnation, in my moments of loneliness and brokenness, has been the strong medicine I need to soothe and heal my heart, and I trust it will be yours as well."
**Cathe Laurie,** Founder and Executive Director, Virtue Women's Ministry

"*Found in Him* is a timely paean to the timeless good news of Christ's incarnation and our union with him. As with everything Elyse writes, it brims with humility and imagination, and the focus on grace is sharp and undeviating. She never flinches from honesty about who we are, which only makes the 'comfort and joy' of what Jesus has done on our behalf that much greater. Would that more of us had her courage (and good humor)!"
**David Zahl,** Executive Director, The Mockingbird Ministries

"This book is a celebration of the person and work of Jesus. Elyse wisely and winsomely shows us the deep wonders of what it means to be found in Jesus. Her theological maturity enables her to write with profound simplicity. This is a book to be savored. Read it slowly, and stop often to worship the one who found you and made you his own. Then read it again."

**Susan Hunt**, Former Director of Women's Ministries for the PCA; author, *Women's Ministry in the Local Church*

"This new book by Elyse warms my heart. She beautifully elaborates on Christ and who he is and what he has accomplished for us. In the later half of *Found in Him*, she shows us how to apply and live out this Good News. Expect your life to change."

**Charles Morris**, speaker; President, HAVEN Today

"It's hard for me to capture how thankful I am for this book. As Elyse is so skilled at doing, she has taken the doctrine of our union with Christ, which sits and collects dust on the shelves of most Christians' theology and has little impact on their living, and displayed for us the beauty of its transformative power. When you don't understand the essential provisions that have been made for you in your union with Christ, you sadly spend your life shopping for what is already yours in him. I will recommend and give away this book again and again and will celebrate with new enthusiasm that I have been found in him!"

**Paul David Tripp**, President, Paul Tripp Ministries; author, *What Did You Expect? Redeeming the Realities of Marriage*

"Resist the temptation to think that a book on the incarnation of Christ and our union with him couldn't help but be dull, dry, and doctrinally abstract. Elyse Fitzpatrick couldn't be dull if she tried! This is a rich, incisive, thoroughly scriptural, and heart-warming journey into the gospel of who Jesus is and what he has done to unite us to himself. Elyse's portrait of Jesus and our life in him will do more than challenge and inform; it will awaken awe at the depths of God's grace and stir adoration for the one who loved you and gave himself for you. Read and rejoice! I did."

**Sam Storms**, Senior Pastor, Bridgeway Church, Oklahoma City

"As Elyse says in this book, there is truly a feast to be found in understanding and meditating on the truth of our union with Christ. This doctrine has transformed how I understand myself and empowered me in healthy relationships with others. Elyse's *Found in Him* is a beautiful exploration of these truths, and I am excited that this resource is now available."

**Wendy Horger Alsup**, mother; author, *Practical Theology for Women* and *The Gospel-Centered Woman*

"*Found In Him* offers a deep but nevertheless eminently practical look at the doctrine of union with Christ. Whether in his union with humanity by virtue of the incarnation or through indwelling the believer by the Holy Spirit, all Christians should know Christ, the one to whom they are united. This book is an able guide to understanding these glorious truths."

**J. V. Fesko**, Academic Dean and Professor of Systematic and Historical Theology, Westminster Seminary California

"One of my favorite experiences was eating at a chocolate buffet at the Cailler chocolate factory, in Broc, Switzerland. Reading Elyse's new book, *Found in Him*, reminded me of that day. Our sister has spread the table with the richest of gospel fare and has invited us to behold, feast, and savor every good thing we have in Christ. This is the finest meditation I have ever read on the radical implications of the incarnation of Christ and our 'this-changes-everything' union with him. Highly accessible, theologically sound, and eminently encouraging, Elyse has once again clearly demonstrated that there's nothing more *than* the gospel, there's just more *of* the gospel."

**Scotty Smith**, Teacher in Residence, West End Community Church, Nashville

"In her treatment of the incarnation of Christ and our union with him, Elyse Fitzpatrick has given us an insightful and compelling presentation of these insufficiently celebrated truths. And she sets them forth not just as truths but as realities that profoundly touch our daily lives—truths which are, in fact, meant to touch our lives deeply and powerfully. To paraphrase Elyse, 'O how impoverished our souls will be if we neglect these sweet doctrines.' I have often told students to read books that make you want to read your Bible more. Here is such a book. I turned often to my Bible, with great joy, while reading *Found in Him*."

**Mike Bullmore,** Senior Pastor, Crossway Community Church, Bristol, Wisconsin

"Elyse Fitzpatrick's writings are always saturated with gospel grace, understanding, and wisdom, and *Found in Him* is no different. With clarity and warmth Elyse meditates on how God answers our isolation and enters into our suffering through the incarnation of Jesus. In Christ we are not alone, and we are part of something much bigger than ourselves. I am thankful for Elyse's ministry and for this book."

**Justin S. Holcomb,** Episcopal priest; Adjunct Professor of Theology and Philosophy, Reformed Theological Seminary, Orlando; author, *On the Grace of God*

"Many of us, if we are honest, have an image of God as the one who is far above us and far away from us. Few of us know our Trinitarian God as so close to us that he is in us and we are in him. My friend Elyse Fitzpatrick takes the doctrine of the incarnation and teaches us that we are not alone—God is with us! Elyse then takes the doctrine of our union with Christ and shows us the soul-altering significance of our connection and communion with God in Christ. *Found in Him* is not just theology come alive, it is theology for life—for your life and mine."

**Robert W. Kellemen,** Vice President and Dean, Faith Bible Seminary, author, *Equipping Counselors for Your Church*

Other Crossway books by Elyse Fitzpatrick:

*Comforts from Romans: Celebrating the Gospel One Day at a Time*, 2013

*Give Them Grace: Dazzling Your Kids with the Love of Jesus* (with Jessica Thompson), 2011

*Counsel from the Cross: Connecting Broken People to the Love of Christ* (with Dennis E. Johnson), 2009

*Comforts from the Cross: Celebrating the Gospel One Day at a Time*, 2009

*Because He Loves Me: How Christ Transforms Our Daily Life*, 2008

# FOUND IN HIM

## THE JOY *of the* INCARNATION *and* OUR UNION *with* CHRIST

### ELYSE M. FITZPATRICK

WHEATON, ILLINOIS

**Library of Congress Cataloging-in-Publication Data**

Fitzpatrick, Elyse, 1950–
   Found in Him : the joy of the Incarnation and our union with Christ / Elyse M. Fitzpatrick.
      pages cm.
   Includes bibliographical references and index.
   ISBN 978-1-4335-3323-5
   1. Incarnation. 2. Mystical union. I. Title.
BT220.F45     2013
232'.1—dc23                       2013005890

Crossway is a publishing ministry of Good News Publishers.

CH        29   28   27   26   25   24   23   22   21   20   19

To
Julius Baxter Fitzpatrick (1916-2012)
Thelma Louise Fitzpatrick (1924-2012)
Dear Parents, Dearly Missed
A day will come when we will be reunited,
Whole, laughing, and never to be separated again.

# Contents

# Acknowledgments

I am thankful to so many people, for God has used so many friends and acquaintances to bring me to the place in my thought wherein I would be able to write this book. I will mention a few of them now but will undoubtedly miss others I should name. God knows.

I am particularly thankful for the very dear pastoral staff of my church, Valley Center Community Church, in Valley Center, California, and in particular for John Sale and David Wojnicki, pastors and dear friends with whom I shared several meals while we were striving together to understand something more about the incarnation. These men, my leaders, were always willing to talk, to pray, to answer questions, to help me judge what I was thinking, and to gently correct. Thank you.

I am also very thankful for Rod Rosenbladt, professor of theology at Concordia University, Irvine, California, for so kindly answering e-mails and directing my study; and to Faith Lutheran Church in San Juan Capistrano, California, who posted his lectures on Martin Chemnitz's unparalleled treatise, *The Two Natures in Christ* (first published 1578), for free viewing on their website. Thank you.

I am also indebted to Scotty Smith, kind friend, who directed me not only to Athanasius's seminal work, *On the Incarnation*, but also to Thomas F. Torrance's marvelous and profoundly illuminating lectures, *Incarnation: The Person and Life of Christ*. Michael Scott Horton was willing to interact with me on a number of occasions, and his work, not only his writings on union with Christ but also his instructive broadcasts on the *White Horse Inn*, have shaped much of what you will read here. I am also thankful for Lutheran Public Radio and the *Issues, Etc.* broadcast; particularly their deeply transformative discussions on the incarnation and life with Christ.

In addition, I'm very thankful for J. Todd Billings's *Union with Christ* and both of Robert Letham's books, *Union with Christ* and *The Work of Christ*. In addition, I'm very grateful to Scott Lindsay and his help in acquainting me with the wonderful resources to be found in Logos 5 software and to Al Fisher and Lydia Brownback, Amy Kruis, and Angie Cheatham, dear friends and cheerleaders from Crossway.

I have also been molded by the dear relationships that God has blessed me with in my personal life. I have learned from Tullian Tchividjian to be generous and zealous and to love the gospel of grace ever more fervently; from my dear friends Julie, Donna, Anita, Rondi, and Kimm; and from our gospel community group, especially Matt and Margaret Lubien, what grace lived out looks like; and from my children's families what grace in deep relationship means (James and Michelle, Jessica and Cody, Joel and Ruth, and, of course, [because I'm the Mimi, I get to put their names in my book] my darlings: Wesley, Hayden, Eowyn, Allie, Gabriel, and Colin).

But most of all, I have learned from my dear husband, Phil, who suffered the loss of both his dear parents, J. B. and Thelma Fitzpatrick, while I was buried in the final stages of labor in the writing of this book, what patient love, understanding, and zeal for Christ's work is. I am blessed.

Great indeed, we confess, is the mystery of godliness:

> He was manifested in the flesh,
>   vindicated by the Spirit,
>     seen by angels,
> proclaimed among the nations,
>   believed on in the world,
>     taken up in glory. (1 Tim. 3:16)

What came back and back to my mind was the thought
of Psyche herself somehow (I never knew well how)
ruined, lost, robbed of all joy, a wailing, wandering shape, for whom I had wrecked everything.

*TILL WE HAVE FACES*, C. S. LEWIS


Who shall separate us from the love of Christ?

ROMANS 8:35

# Introduction

When I was a child, I had a recurring nightmare. I would dream that I was standing on a darkened stage, completely alone. In my dream I wasn't able to move, hide, or even speak. Rooted to the ground in terror, I sensed a threatening presence lurking just out of sight. I was lost, wandering. Somehow, and though I didn't know how then, I knew I was ruined and had ruined something, and that there was nothing I could do to make up for my mistake.

Even now, though I'm in my sixties, I can still feel the isolation and dread that threatened to engulf me on that dark stage. I was completely alone, engulfed with inescapable dread, barely able to breathe. I can't describe how terrifying that felt and still feels to me now when I call it to mind.

If you want to try to psychoanalyze me, I'll admit that I was what today might be called a "latchkey kid," and my nightmare probably expressed that loneliness and my sense that there was something intrinsically wrong with me that wasn't wrong with people who had "normal" families. My dad had left our home fairly early on, and my mom worked hard to try to make ends meet for my brother and me. When I think back on my childhood, "family" isn't a word I would use to describe it. After walking home alone from school every day, I would play by myself (and eat toast) until my mom arrived home from work, usually about 6 p.m. Then we would have some dinner, and I would go play with my dolls by myself or watch TV. My early life wasn't very social. In fact, it really wasn't social at all. I didn't have a lot of friends.

From this, you might conclude that it isn't surprising that I had nightmares about being alone and fatally flawed. That dream was, in some ways, a mirror on a lost and wandering little girl's soul. But I don't think I'm the only one who has ever felt that way. In fact, I think everyone struggles with feelings of alienation and a suspicion that something is very broken at the deepest places in our lives, no matter if we grew up as latchkey kids or in a loving family of nine.

It also seems to me, though, that everyone continues to hope. We hope that someday we'll wake up to discover that we aren't isolated, standing on that darkened stage, awaiting judgment, and that all that dread was just a bad dream after all. We hope that there is something more than this loneliness and isolation, something that will last beyond holiday family dinners and into the night when everyone is gone and we're alone again. On our hope-filled days we are like children waiting to hear some good news—news that will assure us that no matter how alone and ruined we are, someone has loved us, someone has rescued us, and soon we will be truly found.

Right before my twenty-first birthday, the Lord graciously saved me. He saved me from my sin and out of my great need. He saved me from the anger, bitterness, self-deception, and self-hatred that had marred my life up to that point. He saved me from my aloneness, isolation, loneliness, and self-condemnation. And he made me part of his family. I didn't know much about him during those early years, but I knew I finally belonged to someone and that this someone mattered more to me than anything. I knew that I was home. I was family. He had given me faith to believe that I was loved and welcomed, and from that point on, everything began to change.

Although this book isn't about my angst growing up as a lonely child, I want you to know where I'm coming from. I know what loneliness and lostness feel like as a child, and I know what it feels like today. I know that latchkey kids aren't the only ones who experience loneliness; we can be surrounded with family and friends and still feel completely out of sync, alone, isolated. We can stand in the foyer at church, surrounded by hundreds of other believers, and still think we're on our own, the only ones failing to perform, still trying to fit in.

## WE ARE ALONE

Everyone struggles with feelings of alienation and isolation, whether or not we were raised with loads of siblings and very attentive parents. Alienation and aloneness are expressed in many ways. It can be expressed as inadequacy: "I can't do this on my own," or "I never seem to be able to get it right!" (whatever *it* is). It can also be expressed in the lack of being understood: "No one really knows me!" or "Why does everyone always misunderstand me?" Or, of course, it can be expressed as deep loneliness: "I'll never fit in," and "Why can't I make friends like she does?"

Sin has wrought devastation and isolation in all our lives. Our experience of sin, our own and others' against us, has brought separation and alienation to all of us. This separation and alienation originates in our broken relationship with God and flows out from there into broken relationships with one another and even with the created world. No matter how popular we might be, none of us has ever experienced deep unity or authentic union with another. Since the day that our forefather and mother were exiled out of the garden of Eden, we've been lost, trying to get back in, trying to find oneness with each other and the Lord, trying to find communion, our way home. We've been trying to be found. The truth is that without Christ, we are utterly alone, and our attempts to fill our hours with goodies or texting or work or even ministry are simply futile attempts to assure ourselves that things aren't so bad after all. But at the end of the day, in the middle of the night, and at the end of our lives, without the love and work of Jesus Christ, the God-man, we are alone and we know it—and it terrifies us. Every one of us is standing on that darkened stage, condemned, lost and wandering, needing to be found.

## THE TRUTH WE ALL NEED

*Found in Him* has been written because most of us, even though we're Christians, are unaware of the importance of our oneness with Christ (commonly called "union") and his amazing oneness with us (known as the "incarnation"). I suspect that, for most of us, the nearness, or imminence, of Jesus barely enters our consciousness as we face the vicissitudes of daily life on that darkened stage. We neglect the doctrines of incarnation and union to our own deep impoverishment. It's a sad reality that many Christians spend their entire lives wandering around a spiritual wilderness, malnourished, thirsting, and consuming rubbish because they have never feasted on the soul-consoling, heart-transforming, zeal-engendering truth found in the study of the incarnation and union. So I invite you to join with me as we feast on these two often-neglected but beautifully resplendent joys. These joys come directly to us from the one from whom we were estranged, and who alone offers the only antidote to the isolation pandemic we're hoping to escape. He offers us this antidote because he has united in himself both God and man, making one new and completely unique Person, and has united believers with himself, with that Person. We will never know how found, loved, welcomed, and reconciled we are until we see how he has forever taken our nature to himself and has bound us to himself in enduring oneness. God is one with man in Jesus Christ, and we are one with him.

I'll admit up front that we're going to be doing a little theology here. Don't let that frighten you. After all, theology is simply the study of God, and you wouldn't have picked up this book if you weren't interested in knowing more about him. Our study won't consist of obscure propositions or ideas disconnected from daily life. You'll find that these truths will bring life, peace, and joy to your soul. Don't worry—we're all growing in the knowledge of him, and in the knowledge of the Lord there is great satisfaction (Ps. 107:9).

## THE FEAST FOUND IN THE INCARNATION

Here's how we're going to go about our study. The first part of this book, chapters 1–6, will introduce you to the topic of God becoming man, the incarnation. Of course, if you've ever sung a Christmas carol, you're already familiar with the incarnation, but I wonder how much any of us ever think about the events of Bethlehem when we're stuck in traffic or in the hospital or applying for unemployment benefits. Does the fact that the second person of the Trinity became a man so that he could love and save you ever cross your mind? As a woman who believed in the incarnation over forty years ago, I'll admit that I never thought about it much, except at Christmas. I suppose it's the same for most of us. The incarnation is most clearly stated in these precious words from John 1:

> And the Word became flesh and dwelt among us, and we have seen his glory, glory as of the only Son from the Father, full of grace and truth. . . . For from his fullness we have all received, grace upon grace. . . . No one has ever seen God; the only God, who is at the Father's side, he has made him known. (John 1:14, 16–18)

What do John's words mean? We'll spend six chapters considering their meaning, but in summary they mean that Jesus Christ "entered into complete solidarity with us in our sinful existence in order to save us, without becoming himself a sinner."[1] We are not alone. He is Immanuel, *God with us* (Matt. 1:23). *God is with us; we are not alone.*

We also learn about the incarnation from Paul in Colossians 2:9: "For in him the whole fullness of deity dwells bodily." A man who lived over two thousand years ago in Israel is also the second person of the Trinity, who had existed from eternity. He is the God-man. How can this be? It is deep mystery, but it's a mystery we must investigate because the implications of the incarnation cannot be exaggerated. In fact, in the 1500s Martin Chemnitz wrote that when we lose the truth of the incarnation, Jesus "can no longer be our Savior." He calls the incarnation the "greatest and sweetest consolation"[2] that we can know.

It's axiomatic to say that we are alone. We are solitary individuals; we all know that. Not only are we alienated from one another; we are alienated from God. But God has taken action. He became man, becoming one with us so that we would not have to live in deep solitude any longer—and his action opens the door not only to deep communion with him but also with one another.

## THE FEAST FOUND IN UNION WITH CHRIST

In the second part of the book, we'll look into Jesus's union with us as individuals and corporately as his bride, the church. When I say "union," I'm referring to the time Jesus taught that he is the vine and that we are to abide in him. I'm also talking about all those places in the New Testament where the apostles, especially John and Paul, use the words "in Christ" or "with Christ." We'll spend time looking into those little phrases, because it seems to me that when we read our Bibles and come across them, we're tempted to simply gloss over them. They seem to us like little needless appendages. Sure, we know they are there, and we know that they must mean something, but, after all, how important can they be?

For example, in the beginning of the book of Ephesians, Paul refers to our union with Christ eleven times (Eph. 1:3–14)! Notice, as you read, the number of times in just two verses our little phrases "in Christ" or "in him" are included:

> Blessed be the God and Father of our Lord Jesus Christ, who has blessed us in Christ with every spiritual blessing in the heavenly places, even as he chose us in him before the foundation of the world, that we should be holy and blameless before him. (vv. 3–4)

I suspect that the little words "in" and "with" are more important than we know, as John Murray contends:

> Nothing is more central or basic than union and communion with Christ. . . . Union with Christ is really the central truth of the whole doctrine of salvation not only in its application but also in its once-for-all accomplishment in the finished work of Christ.[3]

## A FEAST FOR OUR SOULS

Throughout all ten chapters of this book, I'll be pressing you to see the ways in which these truths relate to you personally by connecting them to real-life examples. But this won't primarily be a book of vignettes. No, I won't waste our time on loads of stories about me, because there is way too much good news to give you, and, after all, my stories, as entertaining as I might think they are, are not what your soul needs.

## THE PLEASURE OF GOD

In closing, here's something more for you to consider: God seems to take great pleasure in union. In fact, God himself is a union of three persons in one God: the Father, the Son, and the Holy Spirit—the Trinity. Consider the following demonstrations of God's love of union in the midst of diversity. Flowing out from God's tri-personal nature we see unity:

*In creation.* God made man in his image (Gen. 1:26).

*In marriage.* First instituted in the garden when man had perfect union with his Creator (Gen. 3:8), and the Creator wanted the man to know the joy of union with someone: "They shall become one flesh" (Gen. 2:24).

*In the incarnation.* The Eternal Word became flesh and dwelt among us (John 1:14).

*In our rebirth.* "He who is joined to the Lord becomes one spirit with him" (1 Cor. 6:17).

*In the church.* "Now you are the body of Christ and individually members of it" (1 Cor. 12:27).

And finally *in our ultimate transformation.* "Just as we have borne the image of the man of dust, we shall also bear the image of the man of heaven" (1 Cor. 15:49).

Because we are made in God's image, we are hardwired to love oneness and fear and despise isolation. It's in our DNA, which is one of the reasons that we're always hoping to find it in relationships or experiences, why we're hoping to get off that dark stage. The fact that even unbelievers love being united with others with a common goal is testimony to that. Need an example? Think NFL. Sixty thousand strangers uniting together in one place to cheer their team on to victory in one voice. There's something more enjoyable about actually being there with others than simply watching it on TV at home alone, isn't there? It's the experience of being a part of something bigger than ourselves and being a part of it with others. I'm no fan of the NFL, but I understand the joys of cheering with thousands of other people in unity.

## THIS IS HOLY GROUND:
## LET US ENTER WITH HUMILITY

The incarnation and Christ's union with us are fundamentally holy mysteries. If we learn of them at all, it will be because he has made us able to know him, and it is his power (not my study or your diligence) that has carried it out. Without his gracious condescension to reveal himself, we would remain completely alone and in the dark. We need the illuminating grace of Christ, and I have prayed and am praying that the Lord will grant us that light.

We cannot earn knowledge of Christ, we cannot achieve it, or build up to it. We have no capacity or power in ourselves giving us the ability to have mastery over this fact. In the very act of knowing Christ, *he is the master, we are the mastered.*[4]

So if we learn anything about him or about our place in his life or his life in us, it is because he is Lord and God, and he has given us revelation of himself. Let us then humbly pray together that his light will shine into our isolation and darkness and that he who spoke light into existence will shine into our hearts to give us "the light of the knowledge of the glory of God in the face of Jesus Christ" (2 Cor. 4:6), our brother, our kinsman-redeemer. We're not standing on that darkened stage alone any more, nor will we ever again—no, now we're standing on holy ground, and we are one with him, our elder brother.

> Long my imprisoned spirit lay
> Fast bound in sin and nature's night;
> Thine eye diffused a quickening ray,
> I woke, the dungeon flamed with light;
> My chains fell off, my heart was free,
> I rose, went forth, and followed Thee.[5]

PART 1

# INCARNATION

# 1

# From Beginning to End
# It's All about Him

*And beginning with Moses and all the Prophets,*
*he interpreted to them in all the Scriptures*
*the things concerning himself.*

LUKE 24:27

The story of Jesus, the long-awaited Christ, is what the entire Bible is about. Perhaps I should say that again. The beginning and end of *everything* in the universe and most particularly everything recorded in the Scriptures is Jesus Christ. He declared himself to be the "Alpha and the Omega," the one "who is and who was and who is to come, the Almighty" (Rev. 1:8). He "is the beginning, the firstborn from the dead." In all that is, he is *"preeminent"* (Col. 1:18). He is the sun around whom all beings orbit, whether they are aware of it or not. He is the director, the author, the actor, and the finale of every act that has ever been played out on humanity's stage.

The man Christ Jesus is the preeminent message of the Bible. Of course there are other messages and secondary peoples and histories, but he's the point of everything that has been written. He is primary; he outranks everyone and everything in importance, dignity, beauty, wisdom, and honor. And because of who he is and what he has done for our salvation,

> God has highly exalted him and bestowed on him the name that is above every name, so that at the name of Jesus every knee should bow, in heaven and on earth and under the earth, and every tongue confess that Jesus Christ is Lord, to the glory of God the Father. (Phil. 2:9–11)

I suppose that those of you who have been Christians for any length of time are nodding in assent. Yes, of course Jesus is the main character in the Bible! That's obvious, isn't it? Well, yes, it should be obvious. But while many of us would agree that Jesus is key, the all-encompassing message of his preeminence, although assumed, is not usually the message we hear. No, the message we usually hear is something about us and what we're supposed to do to make God happy, or, at least, about how we can avoid making him unhappy and live satisfying lives. But as we'll learn in the chapters to come, the Bible isn't primarily a rulebook, nor is it a self-help manual; it's not about how we become better people so that we can earn blessings by working hard. It's all about Jesus, *God made man*, his life, death, and resurrection. It is about his determination to be in union with us.

The message of the Bible is Jesus Christ, the one truly good human person: who he is and the work he's done for our salvation and his Father's glory. Of course, what he has done does intersect with our lives and change us, but we're not the subject of this story—he is. He is the subject, and all the verbs are about his work. But this story didn't start a mere two thousand years ago in Bethlehem.

## THE SON BEFORE THE BABY

Way before the Christmas story was written, the Bible resounded with the message of the Son. In fact, all of the Old Testament writings are about Jesus. Every law, every prophetic utterance, every narrative, every psalm is meant to remind us of him, to force us to look away from ourselves and to look to him for salvation.

Adam's, Abraham's, and Israel's entire experience was designed from the beginning to foreshadow the end [that] . . . Jesus, the beloved Son, would keep the covenant and bear the curse on their behalf and ours.[1]

In fact, Jesus himself claimed that he was the subject of all of Israel's history. I know that this might be a new thought for some of you, so here are some passages from the New Testament for your consideration. Notice how Jesus identifies himself as the subject of all of Moses's writings:

> You search the Scriptures because you think that in them you have eternal life; *and it is they that bear witness about me.* . . . If you believed Moses, you would believe me; *for he wrote of me.* (John 5:39, 46)[2]

Think of that! Jesus said that Moses actually wrote about him! But that's not all he had to say on the topic. After the crucifixion and resurrection, Jesus appeared to his disciples on the road to Emmaus and taught them (and by extension, us) the right way to read and interpret all the Old Testament Scriptures:[3]

> These are my words that I spoke to you while I was still with you, *that everything written about me in the Law of Moses and the Prophets and the Psalms must be fulfilled.* (Luke 24:44)

> And beginning with *Moses and all the Prophets,* he interpreted to them in all the Scriptures *the things concerning himself.* (Luke 24:27)

## EVEN BEFORE THE AGES BEGAN

Jesus (and the rest of the New Testament writers) made it abundantly clear that all the history contained in the Old Testament was ultimately about him: his person and his work. But even further back, even before Genesis 1 and the first light of creation, he was already involved in our salvation. His preeminence in our salvation didn't start when Adam and Eve were created or even when they first sinned. Although Jesus the God-man doesn't actually appear until his physical birth in Bethlehem around two thousand years ago, God the Son, the second person of the Trinity, had existed in communion with God the Father and God the Spirit eternally. From before the Word was spoken and the Holy Spirit hovered over the womb of the unformed world (Gen. 1:2), God the Son existed in inexpressible light and endless joy in union and loving fellowship with his Father and the Spirit. The Son, the personal Word, was "with" God and was, in fact, God (John 1:1–2; 1 John 1:1).

There, in time, before time began, the Trinity existed in perfect happiness within his person. He was not lonely; he never needed anything. In himself, God the Father, God the Son, and God the Spirit were absolutely complete, a Trinity existing in perfect harmony and unity. But then, in overflowing love, grace, and mercy, God chose to make a covenant within himself, sometimes called the *pactum salutis* or covenant of redemption.[4] In it the Son agreed to be sent as a redeemer for a race of men yet to be created, but in order to do so, he would have to become a new sort of person, one in the likeness of his fallen brothers and yet immutably God. He agreed to do this not out of necessity, not because he was forced to or lacked something in himself that only the incarnation would provide, but because of God's "own purpose and grace, which he gave us in Christ Jesus *before the ages began*" (2 Tim. 1:9).

Now, before we look more deeply at what that means, why not take a moment to think a bit more about it? Consider this: before the ages began it was God's plan to come to you, to call you to himself, to save you and make you his own. Though you were lost, he set out to find you and make you one with him. He wasn't shocked or taken by surprise by Adam's fall in Eden. Before the ages began he had already planned for it. He is not shocked or surprised by your weakness or sin. He saw it all before you were ever born and yet purposed to come to you with his grace—not in judgment, but in lavish grace.

Our sin and salvation didn't necessitate a plan B. His purpose to bring salvation before the ages began is now and always has been the only plan there ever was. Our sin didn't paint him into a corner or leave him scrambling to try to fix the big mess we had made. We were chosen "in him before the foundation of the world" (Eph. 1:4).

## IN ALL-KNOWING LOVE THE LORD CREATED

In love God made mankind, knowing what it would cost him, knowing all about Bethlehem and Calvary and all our sins before they even existed. In joy he said, "Let us make man in our image, after our likeness" (Gen. 1:26). By his Son, the creative Word, he made "all things" (John 1:3), including man, and gave him life by personally breathing into him his first breath. So Adam and Eve were created—perfect creatures in perfect love and harmony with each other and with their creator, the Son, who would visit them for joyous walks in the "cool of the day" (Gen. 3:8).

But this bliss would not last. Soon the couple would know the bitter taste of conflict, disunity, and isolation; they would be sent wandering and weeping away from the garden, and they would know that without a doubt this was their own doing.

The Serpent tempted them by questioning the very love of God for them that was at the heart of their creation.

*"If God really loved you he would let you eat of the tree of knowledge of good and evil,"* he hissed. *"Go ahead; help yourself. That way there won't be any difference between you and him. In fact, you'll be just like him. Take care of yourself. You can do it!"*

The Lord had wisely fashioned Adam and Eve in his own image for fellowship with him and with each other, and, oh, the madness of craving something other. Of course, they knew that what they had in communion with their creator and each other was great (even though there were differences), but they were captivated by the thought of how much better life would be if there weren't any differences at all! They didn't want to be creatures any more—they wanted to be gods, too! They knew about goodness already, but they didn't know about evil, and they were so curious. Wouldn't it be a good thing for them to know everything there was to know? Didn't they need to help themselves out?

Adam and Eve drank from the poisonous cup of autonomy and independence. They ate and fell. They fell from their blessed communion with the Lord and were banished from the beautiful garden he had created for them. They fell also from blessed union with each other. God's image in them was shattered (though not completely obliterated), and in that shattering every relationship within the race of man would thereafter be marred. On our own, we would never know the "oneness" we all long for. Where once Adam and Eve had been "one flesh," now they were individuals. Where once they had been self-forgetful, now each was "turned in upon himself. . . . Each [knew] that he or she was no longer what he or she ought to be."[5] They experienced shame. They hid. They tried to cover themselves with fig leaves; they wept in isolation.

Notice that Adam immediately began to refer to himself in the singular "I" rather than as "we" (Gen. 3:10). The deathly individualization of humanity had begun, and with surprising ease Adam deserted his wife while casting aspersions upon the Lord's wisdom for giving her to him in the first place. Adam was utterly alone. He had abandoned his wife. He no longer trusted his God. On her own, Eve was weak and vulnerable. And though we are no longer hiding behind a tree in that garden, the die had been cast for the rest of us. All their children, all of us, will hide from each other and the Lord in isolation, suspicion, and shame, trying to weave together fig leaves to cover our shame.

## SEPARATION AND DEATH

Before Adam and his wife left the garden from which they had been banished, God cursed them and told them of the enmity and conflict that would forever plague them. There would be enmity between mankind, animals, and the created earth, between the wife and her husband. The evening walks with the Son would end (for now). Man was alone, isolated, solitary, lost.

Thankfully, that isn't the end of the story. Although the Lord had spoken a curse of death for disobedience, he also comforted them with good news. Eve would be a mother. Through the woman a child would come who would bruise or crush the Serpent's head (Gen. 3:15; Rom. 16:20). Even in the devastation that their sin had caused, there was still good news: there would be new life, off-spring, another Man who would comfort his mother, who would be born from her and who would be uniquely created in God's image. He would walk in the evening with his people and talk with them about the inevitability and blessing of another tree. The enemy would be vanquished. And as a foreshadowing of this new Man's life and death, God clothed Adam and Eve with the skins of animals: living, breathing creatures were slaughtered to cover their nakedness and shame.

## BEFORE ABRAHAM WAS, I AM

In astounding grace, God called a descendant of Adam and Eve, Abraham, out of Ur, a land of idol worshipers. God promised that through Abraham all the families of the earth would be blessed (Gen. 12:3); that is, through Abraham's offspring, namely, Jesus, God would again come to his people, but this time in a way that no one could have foreseen (Gal. 3:16). God's Son would become a man! A miracle birth would occur, and this Promised One would eventually give his life as ransom for the blessing of many, fulfill-ing God's ancient promise to Abraham (Acts 3:25). Abraham was one of the greatest men in the Old Testament, but his story is not meant to focus us on him or his goodness or his life. Yes, we are to follow in his faith, but Abraham isn't the point of the story. Jesus, the one in whom Abraham believed, is.

Abraham trusted in Jesus! How could that happen? After all, Abraham lived and died thousands of years before Jesus was even born. Jesus knew that he was the ultimate fulfillment of his Father's ancient promise to Abraham. Thousands of years after the promise of blessing had been given to Abraham, Jesus shocked his listeners by declaring that Abraham had seen "his day" and had been gladdened by it. Jesus tells us that Abraham knew him because this man, Jesus, had existed before him. His hearers incredulously asked, "You are not yet fifty years old, and have you seen Abraham?" Jesus said to them, "Truly, truly, I say to you, before Abraham was, I am" (John 8:57–58).[6]

In using the phrase "I am," Jesus was declaring that not only had he existed before his actual physical birth in Bethlehem, but also that he was Yahweh himself. That his hearers understood exactly what he meant is shown by their response to his words: "So they picked up stones to throw at him" (John 8:59). They were infuriated because Jesus was proclaiming that God had been furnished with a body and a soul and that they were looking at God in the flesh! His audacity was too much to bear. His blasphemy had to be silenced.

## TWO MIRACLE BIRTHS, TWO BLOODY MOUNTAINS

After many years and numerous trials, the Lord finally granted aged Abraham and his elderly wife, Sarah, a beloved son, Isaac. This miracle son, born to a father who was "as good as dead," and a mother who was "past the age" (Heb. 11:11–12), would ultimately be offered up as a sacrifice on Mount Moriah. The wood for the sacrifice was laid on Isaac's back while he and his father made the journey up the mountain with knife and fire (see Genesis 22).

Like Isaac before him, Jesus too would carry the wood for his sacrifice as he walked up Calvary, probably the same mountain that Abraham had walked up before him. And there, like Isaac, Jesus willingly lay down on the wood to die. But although Abraham was willing to offer the son he loved as a sacrifice, there could only be one promised Son offered up by the loving Father, so it is here that the similarities between Mount Moriah and Calvary ended.

Isaac would never know the thrust of his father's knife, but our Lord experienced far more than that—his wrists, ankles and side were pierced for our transgressions (Isa. 53:5). Isaac would never gape in wonder at his father's desertion, but the Son would cry out, "My God, my God, why have you forsaken me?" (Matt. 27:46). At the very moment when the Father should have freed Jesus from his captivity, as Abraham had freed Isaac, the Father poured out all his fiery wrath upon him. Jesus was the ram who was "caught in a thicket" (Gen. 22:13) and slaughtered on a mount so that we could go free. He was caught in the thicket of our sin, but this was no accident. He willingly walked into it and became "sin" (2 Cor. 5:21) and a "curse" (Gal. 3:13) for us so that we might be eternally his. The perfect incarnate Son is the only offering who can atone for sin—for Abraham's, Isaac's, and ours. No matter how hard we work, we cannot atone for our sin or make it up to God. Jesus alone is the Lamb who takes away the sins of the world. Now Abraham's experience becomes ours, and we, like him, meet Jehovah-Jireh, the God who provides on the "mount of the LORD" (Gen. 22:14). In Christ, Jehovah-Jireh has provided all we need: a savior, a redeemer, a friend and a husband. We are no longer alone, trying to offer sacrifices that prove our love and fidelity. We are his. We have been found.

## JESUS: THE PROPHET GREATER THAN MOSES

God prospered Abraham and his son Isaac and grandson Jacob. Jacob grew to become a great family, known by Jacob's new name, Israel. During a time of famine the family went down to Egypt under Jacob's son Joseph's care, and there the family multiplied into a great nation. Soon they were forced into slavery by a ruler who did not "know" Joseph (Ex. 1:8), but God delivered his people out of Egypt through great plagues and wonders by the hand of a deliverer, Moses. Even Moses knew that he wasn't the point of the story, though God used him greatly. He knew that there would be a greater true Deliverer who would come after him and of whom he foretold:

> The LORD your God will raise up for you a prophet like me from
> among you, from your brothers. . . . And I will put my words in
> his mouth, and he shall speak to them all that I command him.
> (Deut. 18:15, 18)

Jesus said that he was the greater prophet Moses had spoken
of. He was raised up from among his brothers, from the Jews,
for all mankind. Jesus fulfilled the words of Moses's prophecy by
speaking the words that were given to him by his Father (John
17:8), doing nothing on his own authority but speaking only as the
Father had taught him (John 8:28). The apostles, too, recognized
that Jesus was the prophet foreshadowed by Moses, the prophet
raised up from among his brothers, the prophet to whom the
people should listen (Acts 3:22–24; 7:37). As great as Moses was,
he was not the deliverer that the people needed.

Because of Israel's stubborn unbelief, they were forced to
wander in the wilderness for forty years. But they were never
truly alone because the true Deliverer never abandoned them. As
they wandered, the Father fed them the bread of heaven. Jesus
said that his flesh was that bread (John 6:32–33, 56–58). Even
more shockingly, Paul tells us that Jesus was the rock that flowed
with water who followed them throughout their wanderings:
"They drank from the spiritual Rock that followed them, and
*the Rock was Christ*" (1 Cor. 10:3–4). He is the water that is sent
for those who are thirsty (John 7:37), and at his final Passover
celebration with his disciples, a celebration that has become the
sacrament of Communion for us, Jesus declared that it is his body
and blood that we are eating and drinking (Matt. 26:26–28). He
has been guiding, sustaining, and feeding his people for eons:
throughout all our wanderings, he has remained faithful to nourish and cherish us (Eph. 5:29), even when our wandering is due
to our unbelief. Jesus was there with Abraham on Mount Moriah
and with the nation of Israel as they thirsted in the wilderness.
And he is here with us today. Jesus is the central figure of all of
Israel's history.

## ROCK OF AGES

God called Moses up onto Mount Sinai and gave him the Law, "written with the finger of God" (Ex. 31:18; certainly another reference to the Son).[7] The people were to live by that law but, of course, they didn't. As was Satan's practice, in the wilderness he tempted them. Would they believe that God would provide? Did he really love them? You know they disbelieved and failed miserably. Having grown tired of waiting for Moses's return from the mountain, the people "sat down to eat and drink and rose up to play" (Ex. 32:6). Upon his return, Moses threw down the stone tablets of the Law, shattering them in pieces, as a sign of what the people had already done. The Lord declared his purpose to obliterate the nation and spare Moses, but Moses interceded on their behalf, and God relented, inviting Moses back up on Mount Sinai to receive the Law from him a second time. Moses's intervention is another beautiful type of the Deliverer to come. But Moses isn't the Savior. No, he needed a deliverer himself.

At this point, Moses made a very bold and loving request. He asked the Lord, "Please show me your glory" (Ex. 33:18). So God allowed Moses to ascend the mountain once again and lovingly placed him in the cleft or fissure of a rock, covering him with his hand so that his glory might pass by him. God enabled Moses to see him without being killed by the sight. Moses was hidden in a broken rock and was given an audible description of God's character:

> The LORD passed before him and proclaimed, "The LORD, the LORD, a God merciful and gracious, slow to anger, and abounding in steadfast love and faithfulness, keeping steadfast love for thousands, forgiving iniquity and transgression and sin, but who will by no means clear the guilty, visiting the iniquity of the fathers on the children and the children's children, to the third and the fourth generation." (Ex. 34:6–7)

Does the broken rock that protected Moses from God's glory have a name? Yes, of course. The Son is the rock of ages who was cleft for us, in whom we are to hide to be protected from what would be a deadly holiness. How are we protected? By the very hand of God. In fact, we are hidden *in* God *from* God by the Son's life, death, and resurrection.[8] We can look upon Jesus, the one in whom the whole fullness of God dwells, and not be killed by the sight. He is the Deliverer. He is the point of the story.

In penning Israel's history, Moses knew that he was writing about something more than himself and his people. He knew that there was a deeper truth he was proclaiming. He was looking forward to another deliverer, to one who didn't need to hide from God. He was looking forward to the rock who would also be a man.

On this side of the incarnation, we can see God's glory face-to-face in the human face of Jesus. We no longer have to worry about being obliterated by his greatness, for he has come to us as Jesus, veiled or cloaked in our flesh, as John writes:

> And the Word became flesh and dwelt among us, and we have seen his glory, glory as of the only Son from the Father, full of grace and truth. . . . No one has ever seen God; the only God, who is at the Father's side, he has made him known. (John 1:14, 18)

## TRUE SALVATION LIFTED UP

In an evening conversation with Nicodemus the Pharisee, Jesus applied another story from Israel's history to himself and his role of Savior. He said, "As Moses lifted up the serpent in the wilderness, so must the Son of Man be lifted up, that whoever believes in him may have eternal life" (John 3:14–15). Nicodemus would certainly have been very well aware of the account of the fiery serpents in the wilderness, God's judgment, and ultimate deliverance of his grumbling people through the brazen serpent (Num. 21:4–9). And undoubtedly, Nicodemus would have turned this piece of history into a morality tale about the ills of complaining—which is the way we all tend to interpret Scripture. Instead of interpreting it in that way, though, Jesus made it an illustration about his ultimate plan to atone for sin by being "lifted up" as the brazen serpent in the wilderness had been. We make this story about us and how we can avoid snakebites. Jesus made it about him and his work.

Nicodemus would never have interpreted the story of the fiery serpents in that way; he would have understood it as God's judgment on grumblers for unbelief and as a warning not to complain. Instead, Jesus used it to turn Nicodemus's trust away from himself through his own ability to avoid complaining and onto his Messiah.

First, he did this by demolishing his confidence in his ability to rightly interpret Scripture and then, by implication, showing him that he could not merit eternal life. Jesus taught him that everything he thought he knew about the sacred Scriptures had been misinterpreted, and then he completely demolished his self-confidence by commanding him to be "born again" (John 3:3), something that Nicodemus instantly realized he could not do. How was Nicodemus supposed to do that? Climb back into his mother's womb? Impossible—yes, and that was the point!

## IT'S NOT ABOUT US—IT NEVER HAS BEEN

Like Nicodemus's contemporaries and ours, the easiest way to interpret the Bible is to make it about us and what we need to do. We take the stories of Abraham, Moses, David, Jonah, and Job and turn them in toward us and make them about how we're supposed to earn God's blessings. But Jesus has a completely different take on them. He taught that all of the Old Testament was meant to point forward to the Christ, to the one who would live a perfect life and die a substitutionary death in our place. If the Old Testament and the history of the nation of Israel has taught us anything, it is that having God's law and knowing that you are special to him won't automatically make you obedient. Israel had both of these privileges and yet failed time and time again; failing finally by refusing to recognize the Messiah, the only one who could save them from their deathly inward curvature. The history of Israel (and the whole world) tells us that fallen humanity is completely unable to do what needs to be done and that something or someone more is needed (Deut. 29:4). We need a true sacrifice, the foretold Deliverer, the water, the bread, the wine, the Rock.

Are you beginning to see how the Son is the underlying story behind every story? Out of love for his people, for all of us who have spent our lives trying to get away from him, living as we pleased, trying to prove that we're really good enough and don't need him, suffering in isolation and wandering, God created man in his own image once again, but this time, this Man would not fail to love or obey him.

When we see Jesus portrayed on the pages of the New Testament, we're seeing God the Son who has been with his people from the very beginning, even from before Malachi or even Genesis, and is now with us not only in types or shadows but has actually become one with us, one of us! Yes, he had been with us all along, but now the Word has become flesh and actually lived like one of us, with us!

What we're about to learn in the incarnation has no parallel in nature or our natural understanding. What we're about to learn in the incarnation is not something that we can learn outside of the work of the Spirit and the condescension of the God-man, Jesus Christ, who has shown himself to us. If you're able to understand it and believe in some small way that everything is really all about him and the work he's done, that's only because God has gifted you with faith. Oh, glorious gift of faith to believe! So let there be "no patting yourself on the back here. Falling on your knees in humility is rather the appropriate response."[9]

So let us do that now. Let us approach our study of the incarnate Christ, who has been with us forever and will be with us eternally, with humility, joy, and trust. If you know who he is, it's because he wants you to know him. You are right now what you have always been: his beloved child for whom he has given everything. He is with you, and you are his beloved; it's all about him and he has found you.

## FOUND IN HIM

At the end of every chapter you'll find a few questions meant to spur on your thinking. Please take time to complete them, and while these thoughts are fresh, write a four- or five-sentence summary of what you've learned here.

1) Why does Jesus's presence with us matter? How much do you struggle with feeling alone or alienated?

2) What does Paul mean when he writes that Jesus is preeminent? Have you ever thought about Jesus being preeminent in the Old Testament before?

3) Which one of the Old Testament narratives in which Jesus is present means the most to you? Why?

4) How does seeing Jesus as the subject of the whole Bible change how you interpret the Bible?

5) In four or five sentences, summarize this chapter.

# 2

# Come Adore on Bended Knee

*But when the fullness of time had come, God sent forth his Son,*
*born of woman, born under the law, to redeem those who were*
*under the law, so that we might receive adoption as sons.*

GALATIANS 4:4–5

Part of what it means to be a Christian is to believe the unbelievable: that the historical human person, Jesus, who was born in a
stable in a backwater village outside of Jerusalem some two thousand years ago, was actually God in the flesh. This inconceivable
proposition, the incarnation,[1] means that, beginning at his birth,
the human baby named Jesus was "fully God and fully man in one
person, and will be so forever."[2] God became man—forever. That
infant in the cradle was Immanuel, God with us!

Paul expressed the incarnation in this way: "In him the whole
fullness of deity dwells bodily" (Col. 2:9). Think of that! Jesus
wasn't just some special appearance of God, a theophany. Nor
was he merely a misunderstood teacher of love who ended up
getting crucified. He was God in the flesh—immortal; invisible
spirit clothed with human hair, skin, and blood; and supported
by muscle and bone. In his humiliation, God had to breathe, eat,
drink, and sleep. When cut he bled. He longed for companionship
and truly suffered when his friends deserted him. He is one of

our kind, and as we "share in flesh and blood, he himself likewise partook of the same things" (Heb. 2:14).

To this day he remains one of us. This truth is the "foundation for all our comfort" *forever*.[3] The incarnation brings unceasing hope and an end to our exile, wandering, and despair. There is great comfort for our souls in the truth that he is just like us. Here's why: the incarnation tells us that even though we sin, we are not alone; even though we're weak and finite, he knows what weakness and mortality are because he was weak and mortal just like us; and even though we continually fail, he has committed himself to be part of a race of failures—and he has done so forever. He does not use our flesh merely as an impersonal dwelling place, like some seedy motel room he can't wait to vacate; rather, he assumes our nature completely and will be the God-man forever, throughout eternity!

## HE IS ONE OF US

The incarnation sets Christianity apart from every other religion. The thought that God would become man is simply without parallel in any other faith. In no other religion does a god do anything more than tell his subjects what to do to become like him, earn his favor, or give instruction on how, if they're lucky, they might avoid ticking him off. In no other religion does a creator god become weak and an indistinguishable part of his creation.

In the incarnation, God became so completely one of us that the people who lived with him didn't notice anything special about him; Jesus's deity was perfectly veiled in human flesh. In fact, when he went to his own village, Nazareth, "the people who had known him for many years did not receive him."[4] "Is not this the carpenter's son?" they asked. "Is not his mother called Mary?" (Matt. 13:55). Even his own family didn't know he was the incarnate one. Think of this: "Not even his brothers believed in him" (John 7:5).

What did Jesus look like? A regular Joe. His form was just

like ours. Put this book down for a moment and look across the room at someone. That's how ordinary he looked. Or, better yet, look at yourself in a mirror. He looked just like you! He had eyes, pores, hair, and teeth. If you'd seen him, you wouldn't have thought he was anything special. He didn't have any sort of magnetism that would make you take a second look. He looked like any twenty- or thirty-something carpenter on any construction job.

His complete identification with us shouldn't have taken his contemporaries by surprise, because seven hundred years before his birth the prophet Isaiah spoke of how normal the Messiah would appear: "He had no form or majesty that we should look at him, and no beauty that we should desire him" (Isa. 53:2). He willingly took a servant's form and was born in the likeness of men. He was fully human (Phil. 2:7–8).

What was baby Jesus like? Did he have some sort of radioactive glow about him? Maybe a little halo or cherubs floating around his head? No. He looked like any Middle Eastern infant, wrapped in rags and nursing at his mother's breast. And contrary to the sweet carol "Away in the Manger," he did cry when awakened by the cattle's lowing. He cried just like us.

Unlike ancient mythological gods, Jesus was no naughty demigod stripped of his superpowers and banished to earth as punishment. Jesus isn't Thor. No, God the Son freely volunteered to become one of us and to forever take to his person all that it meant to be human. "Though he was rich, yet for your sake he [voluntarily] became poor, so that you by his poverty might become rich" (2 Cor. 8:9). The incarnation isn't a punishment on the Son; it is an act of his love, a "voluntary humiliation."[5] He gladly "made himself nothing" (Phil. 2:7 NIV). He who had everything, who was Lord of all, God Most High, creator, became a poor servant—your servant—out of love for you, his beloved. He came to serve you and win you with his love. He became one of our own so that we could be his own.

## JESUS THE JEW

But his self-humiliation didn't end with becoming a human. He was born as a Jew, into the nation of Israel, an insignificant nation that the Lord described in this way:

> It was not because you were more in number than any other people that the LORD set his love on you and chose you, for you were the fewest of all peoples. (Deut. 7:7)

Further, there wasn't any other nation upon which the Lord so incessantly poured his love and yet was so opposed to his wooing. Even though he loved them, they gave themselves completely to wickedness. Nehemiah described Israel's persistent resistance in these terms:

> Nevertheless, they [the Israelites] were disobedient and rebelled against you and cast your law behind their back and killed your prophets, who had warned them in order to turn them back to you, and they committed great blasphemies. Therefore you gave them into the hand of their enemies, who made them suffer. And in the time of their suffering they cried out to you and you heard them from heaven, and according to your great mercies you gave them saviors who saved them from the hand of their enemies. . . . Yet they acted presumptuously and did not obey your commandments, but sinned against your rules, which if a person does them, he shall live by them, and they turned a stubborn shoulder and stiffened their neck and would not obey. (Neh. 9:26–27, 29)

In fact, this nation had a history of being so wicked that even the Philistines, those idolatrous wretches, were actually ashamed of Israel's lewd behavior (Ezek. 16:27). Because of the Israelites' relentless stubbornness and unbelief, they were trodden under the heel of one wicked nation after another, and it was into this nation of failures (in every sense of that word) that the Savior chose to be born, in a Roman colony in a barn where his family had been forced to travel for taxation purposes. In his veins flowed Jewish blood, and in his manhood he remains Jesus the Jew to this day. Jesus the Jew embraces Israel's national identity as the shameful chosen who were not known for their consecration but rather for their idolatry, insignificance, weakness, and slavery. How many times had they suffered exile as punishment for their rebellion? He came unto his own people, but in typical fashion, they "did not receive him" (John 1:11).

He could have come as a wise Chinese, a powerful Roman, or a philosopher Greek, but he didn't. Instead he came as a weak Savior, first to the Jews among whom there were not many wise, not many powerful, not many of noble birth (1 Cor. 1:26), and then to all the Gentile races who would hear the message through them. He was born as Savior for a world full of foolish, weak, ignoble losers. All of Israel's history demonstrates how willing Christ was to be humbled.

This needs to speak to your heart so that you know that no matter what kind of "loser" you are, Jesus willingly condescended to go even lower than that. He had no great pedigree. He was of questionable lineage, working class, uneducated, poor, weak, despised, rejected, and exiled. This is the baby and his family of origin; this is your Savior.

## VEILED IN FLESH THE GODHEAD SEE

The incarnate God-man Jesus Christ is completely matchless, and his condescension to humanity's earthiness, finitude, frailty, and sin should astonish us and provoke worship. But the sad truth is that we've become so very familiar with this story that we can hum carols during the Christmas season while we shop for trinkets and never once fall on our faces in awe. Think on these words:

> Veiled in flesh the Godhead see,
> Hail the incarnate Deity,
> Pleased with us in flesh to dwell
> Jesus, our Emmanuel [God with us].[6]

Consider those words again: the invisible God, the Son, has been "veiled in flesh." How can that be? The nativity story tells us. Similar to the way the Spirit hovered over creation (Gen. 1:2), the Holy Spirit hovered over a willing virgin girl named Mary.[7] And as in the Genesis story, where the Word spoke and life appeared out of lifelessness, so it was in the womb of Mary.

> The Holy Spirit will come upon you, and the power of the Most High will overshadow you; therefore the child to be born will be called holy—the Son of God. (Luke 1:35)

Within the darkness of the virgin's womb, the eternal Word entered an ovum and took to himself from her body chromosomes, blood, flesh, and bone. The Word who was made flesh (John 1:14) gestated within her for nine months. *God relied on a weak young girl to sustain his life.* She ate and drank and nourished this embryo (who is also the Lord of heaven and earth) from the limited resources of her own little body. In his humanity he knew the restraint of living within a uterus, completely confined, in deep darkness. He felt it when his mother labored, and although he did not understand the process, like every infant before him, he struggled to be free and to breathe. He was born, "placenta and all,"[8] as he came forth from the virgin's womb, a strange shrine for our God. He is like us in *every way*; he knows what it is to be born and live our life. We are not alone—you are not alone.

> For we do not have a high priest who is unable to sympathize with our weaknesses, but one who *in every respect* has been tempted as we are, yet without sin. (Heb. 4:15)

Physically, the eternal Word was just like his mother, our sister. He experienced cold and hunger. He needed his diaper changed. Mary nursed him, and his life was sustained by her milk. As he grew, he enjoyed the comfort of his mom's hugs. He loved the smell of her. He giggled when he felt his dad's prickly beard on his cheek. He was kissed and learned to kiss in return. Snuggling felt good to him. Mentally and emotionally, he had a soul just like ours. That meant that he was social; he enjoyed family and friends and felt the sting of rejection. He loved to laugh, and he cried when he experienced discomfort and sorrow. He was sad when he was alone.

As he grew into a toddler, he began to learn language. Think of that! The Word who spoke the universe into existence had to learn Hebrew (and probably Aramaic). He had to learn how to say, "Abba," "Dada." Then he lisped, "I love you," to his earthly mama. She taught him table manners. His dad would read to him from the Torah because he hadn't yet learned to read. He would hear the Prophets, the Psalms, and the Law, and he would grow in his understanding of them until one day when, as an adult, he would realize that every word he had heard had actually been spoken about his life, death, and resurrection. But he didn't instinctively know this as a little child first learning to pronounce the *aleph*.

## HE SHALL BE CALLED "JESUS"

As an eight-day-old he was given the name that the angel had spoken to both Mary and Joseph—*Jesus*. Why "Jesus"? Why not "Joseph"? His name had to be Jesus, *yehôšua*, for, as the angel said, "He will save his people from their sins" (Matt. 1:21; see also John 3:17; 1 Tim. 1:15).[9]

From the very moment of his naming, even from the earliest days of his humanity, Jesus was traversing a road that would unavoidably lead to Calvary's bloody hill. His people needed salvation, and he was born for one reason only: to provide it. But in order to save us, he had to be one of us. Only a man could pay the penalty for our sin; but only God would be free from sin and be able bear up under the unmitigated wrath of God. He had to be God and yet man, one of us, *and he was*.

At that naming ceremony, Jesus the Jew was circumcised. Circumcision is a covenant seal, a sign made in the body of male infants, which was commanded by God and marked them as members of the community God had made promises to. It was a painful and bloody sacrament that symbolized the excision or cutting away of the "guilt and pollution of sin, and obliging the people to let the grace of God penetrate their entire life."[10]

Doesn't it seem wrong for the baby Jesus to be marked like that? If the point of circumcision was the symbolic cutting away of the guilt and pollution of sin, why did Jesus, the holy child (Luke 1:35), have to suffer it? He had no guilt, no original sin that needed to be removed. His body was "formed as was the body of Adam by the immediate agency of God, uncontaminated and without spot or blemish."[11]

Though he was one in a line of sinners, the normal genealogy—"this sinner begat that sinner" (Matt. 1:1–16; Luke 3:23–38)—was interrupted in his conception and birth. Yes, Mary was a sinner, but she was also a virgin, and that's important because we sinners need a completely new sort of person to bring us salvation. None of us, no matter how sweet our little children might seem to us, ever gives birth to anything other than sinners. We are condemned to produce after our own kind. How hopeless our plight!

But Jesus's conception breaks into this deadly heritage. He was unique: he had no earthly father from whom he would inherit guilt "and a corrupt moral nature."[12] The previously unbroken line of sinners giving birth to sinners was gloriously interrupted in Christ. God, not Joseph, was his Father. He was unique in all of history and yet—glorious truth!—he was also wholly one of us, and his life would mark the beginning of a completely new race of men and women. A new race of man had broken in that would produce children after its own kind.

Jesus had to go through everything we go through in order to be our Savior, to be one of us. Even as an infant, in his circumcision, he had to bleed for sins he would never commit. He didn't need this mark of covenant grace in his flesh. *He himself was covenant grace in the flesh.* Even though he was God and could have excused himself from suffering under this rite, he embraced his humanity and did not call out for help to avoid this pain. No, he submitted to it because he had to be one of us in every respect. He bled. He cried. His mother and father comforted him.

## THE BOY CHRIST JESUS

Aside from his birth, circumcision, presentation at the temple, and journey to celebrate Passover at age twelve, the Scripture is mostly silent on his childhood. This may be because there was nothing remarkable about it. For sure, there is nothing from it that we need to know for our salvation, or we would be told. This silence simply proves that the little boy Jesus was just like any other little boy who ever lived—but without sin, of course. If we want to know what he was like, all we need to do is look at our children and imagine what they would be like if they had never sinned, if they didn't have sinners for parents.

There are two specific passages in Luke, however, that shed some light on his maturation, and it is to those two passages we will turn our attention now. The first passage is from Luke 2:40: "And the child grew and became strong, filled with wisdom. And the favor of God was upon him." This passage employs four key words that describe him. These words are "grew," "strong," "wisdom," and "favor."

### THE CHILD GREW

The fact that the child who was God *grew* should amaze us. How can God grow? The fact that he grew doesn't mean that he was imperfect in any way but rather that, in his humanity, he was young and little and needed to mature. Isaiah wrote, "For he grew up before him like a young plant, and like a root out of dry ground" (Isa. 53:2).

The fact that he grew is important because growth is part of our life, too; he's just like us. Our children grow and are not today what they will be ten years from now. Jesus was a child. He needed to mature into adulthood. Childhood is not part of the curse, nor is immaturity necessarily sin. Being unable to foresee every eventuality is not sinful; it is weakness. Jesus had to develop knowledge of how the world worked. His brain needed to form neural connections that weren't there when he was born. He had to grow in understanding the world; he would learn about the seasons and the feel of a sheep before it is sheared. Jesus had to develop skin and bone and muscle. He experienced growing pains at night as his muscles stretched. He lost his baby teeth and would have to be taught the appropriate responses to make when he went to synagogue with his father. He grew in every sense of the word. The boy Jesus at five would have been very similar to any other five-year-old, and he was different from the boy Jesus at twelve. God grew.

## He Became Strong

Think of this—the one who "upholds the universe by the word of his power" (Heb. 1:3) needed to grow in strength. That meant that in his veiled deity, as a child he was weak. When playing games with his friends, he didn't always win. He couldn't lift a heavy water jug, nor could he remember everything that others said to him. He was weak both physically and mentally in the same way that our children are weak and that we are weak. For instance, I can't count the number of times that I walk into a room to get something and can't remember what it was that I came after. This is weakness, and physical weakness is not necessarily the result of sin. As I'm getting older and finding more weakness invading my body, I'm glad that weakness doesn't exclude me from the life of God. I am glad that God was weak. He understands. He forgot things. His body was just like ours. Weakness is not something to be ashamed of. In his humiliation, God was weak and had to grow in strength.

## Filled with Wisdom

The Lord Jesus, "in whom are hidden all the treasures of wisdom and knowledge" (Col. 2:3), had to grow in wisdom. This means that he didn't automatically know all the wisdom of Proverbs. Like the son in Proverbs 1:8, he had to "hear" his father's instruction and "forsake not" his mother's teaching. He also didn't know exactly how that wisdom would mesh with the world in which he lived, nor did he automatically know the place of a specific passage in the Scriptures. He had to learn. Sometimes he was wrong and just didn't know the right answer. Because he intentionally lived only as a human, veiling his omniscience, his ability to foresee the future was just like ours (Mark 13:32).

But because Jesus never fought against God's wisdom and instead always embraced it, it should not surprise us that he was filled with wisdom at a young age. By the time he was just twelve, his wisdom astonished the religious leaders of his day (Luke 2:47). Even so, his growth in wisdom wasn't miraculous; he didn't get any special help from the fact that he was God. He had to learn wisdom just as we do, but he didn't resist it as we do, so he grew wise quickly.

## THE FAVOR OF GOD WAS UPON HIM

From the very beginning of his life, he knew what it was to live with the light of God's countenance upon him. He grew to sense God's smile upon his life, and God's grace invaded every moment of his day. He learned what it was like to please his Father, and although he might not have known exactly who he was at that point, he did know that pleasing the Lord was the most important activity he could pursue. He was righteous, and he was always the happiest child in the room. It is written of him that he

> loved righteousness and hated wickedness; therefore God, your God, has anointed you with the oil of gladness beyond your companions. (Heb. 1:9)

He was happy without being cruel, and good without being a prig.

As a child Jesus grew, became strong, and increased in wisdom, and the favor of God was upon him. What we have learned about him is that he was just like us but then, in one way, he was already beginning to pull away. He lived a sinless life and basked daily in the favor of the God he delighted to please, and none of us naturally knows what that's like. And he smiled a lot—a lot more than we do.

## IN THE TEMPLE

At age twelve Jesus went up to the temple with his family. This journey marked an important milestone in his young life because at twelve,

> according to Jewish law a son passes from infancy to the state of adult responsibility . . . when the child himself confesses with his own lips the word of God sealed in his flesh in circumcision.[13]

In his parents' weakness, they misunderstood Jesus's mission and accused him of mistreating them by staying behind in the temple. Even so, Jesus went back down to Nazareth with his parents and was "submissive" to them (Luke 2:51). Let's not miss the import of this statement. This child, who now was beginning to grow into the man he would be and was beginning to know what he was to do and where he belonged, submitted to their flawed leadership.

Undoubtedly he went up to Jerusalem repeatedly every year after that, but we don't see him in the temple disputing with the leaders again. Why not? Because it wasn't yet time for him to be known publicly. He still had eighteen years of humdrum life as a carpenter to live. Why? For us. Whenever we struggle with submitting to unwise or sinful authority, whenever we feel that we're stuck in some dead-end, mundane life, we can remember that Jesus understands. He sawed wood and hammered nails and swept up shop for eighteen years, learning more and more about who he was and what his ultimate mission was. He knows what it is for you to be stuck in traffic or to change another diaper for the eighth time today. In his life as an ordinary carpenter, learning his trade, being given the jobs that only novices got, he gave boring work value forever.

## HE INCREASED IN OBEDIENCE

Luke summarizes Jesus's early life by saying that "Jesus *increased* in wisdom and in stature, and in favor with God and man" (Luke 2:52). The obedience of Jesus Christ was not light or a sham obedience. It was agonizingly real as he bore our flesh of sin and struggled with our weakness. The word translated "increased" in this verse is an "astonishing word about the growth of Jesus, '*proekopten*,'" which means "that he had to beat his way forward with blows. His obedience was a battle."[14] Just because he never gave into temptation doesn't mean obedience was easy for him; it was more difficult than anything we will ever experience.

Hebrews 5:8 tells us that "although he was a son, he learned obedience through what he suffered." This learning of obedience doesn't mean that he was "learning his lesson" or being punished for wrongdoing. It means that he had to learn how to say yes to God and no to sin every single moment of his earthly life, and this earthly life was, in itself, a suffering for him. His very humiliation as one of us—being cold, hungry, tired, and having to learn truth—was a life of suffering from his earliest days. Ultimately he would learn full obedience, when he submitted in Gethsemane and breathed out his, "Not my will but yours." Because he must be like us in every way, he was born under the law and under the curse of death that Adam, as our representative, brought down on our heads through his disobedience.

Emotionally and spiritually Jesus had a human soul, exactly like ours yet sinless, and he had to struggle to grow in wisdom and obedience. He was pure like Adam had been in the garden before he fell. Like Adam, he knew real temptation, but unlike Adam, he loved his Father and his bride more than he loved himself. He had to grow in obedience, not because he was sinful or had a sin nature but because his life was one of faith, just like ours.

# INCARNATION

## FALL ON YOUR KNEES

What is the appropriate response to the incarnation? As we've looked at the Christmas story, I purposely skipped over the worship that angels, magi, and shepherds brought to him, because I wanted to save it for our last few moments together. I wanted you to begin to experience what they experienced before I bid you worship with them.

### Angels, Shepherds, and Wise Men

Angels are present all over the incarnation story; it's almost as though they're simply beside themselves with wonder and awe. What is their King, the Son they have loved and served for eons, doing breathing air as incarnate man? An angel, Gabriel, brought the announcement of Jesus's birth to Mary and Joseph. Here are the words he used to describe the incarnate one:

> He will be great and will be called the Son of the Most High. And the Lord God will give to him the throne of his father David, and he will reign over the house of Jacob forever, and of his kingdom there will be no end. (Luke 1:32–33)

> Therefore the child to be born will be called holy—the Son of God. (Luke 1:35)

Jesus is great, the Son of the Most High, a King with an everlasting kingdom who will also be *yehôšua*, our Savior (Matt. 1:20–23). He will be called "out of Egypt" so that both Jew and Gentile will have a part in him (2:15). He will be born in Bethlehem, an insignificant hick village that will produce what appears to be just another (as was supposed) bastard child. But this child will rule and gently shepherd his people, Israel (v. 6).

How long has it been since this story was good news of great joy for you (Luke 2:10–11)? Is your heart full of praise? Will you join with the angels and give "glory to God in the highest" (v. 14)? Will you join with the shepherds, glorifying and praising God for what you have been told (v. 20)? Will you rejoice exceedingly with great joy and fall down before the child along with the magi? Will you lay before him the treasure you have been grasping so tightly? Will you notice the gifts, the gold, frankincense, and myrrh? These were gifts meant for a royal baby but were ultimately for embalming our King.

There are simply no words to explain what we have here. We have received a revelation of a mystery that is completely beyond our capacity to comprehend. What is our response? To fall on our knees in worship.

> Give heed, my heart, lift up thine eyes!
> What is it in yon manger lies?
> Who is this child, so young and fair?
> The blessed Christ-child lieth there.
> Welcome to earth, Thou noble Guest,
> Through whom the sinful world is blest!
> Thou com'st to share my misery;
> What thanks shall I return to Thee?[15]

## FOUND IN HIM

1) The incarnation is utter mystery. How can God be both God and man at the same time without losing his God-ness or his man-ness? Even though it is a mystery (and we should be used to mysteries by now—think of the Trinity), we must not let our incomprehension keep us from finding the comfort that it is meant to bring. What to you is the most comforting part of the incarnation? Why?

2) Martin Chemnitz wrote that Satan's goal is to steal the truth of the incarnation away from us. Why would Satan want us to give up in confusion when trying to think about this? How successful has our enemy been in his quest to desensitize or confuse us about the God-man?

3) When Jesus was presented at the temple at about six weeks old, two saints, Simeon and Anna, worshiped him. Look up in Luke 2:29–38 the words they used to describe him and think about why they had the response they did.

4) Mary was told that she was "blessed" above all women but that a sword would "pierce through your own soul" (Luke 2:34–35). In what way does knowing that Mary suffered for her faith, though she was blessed, encourage you today? If you've had children, you know what it is to hold and behold your little baby, to look into his eyes and want the best for him and hope that he will never have to suffer. How does Mary's faith help you today?

5) Even if it is the middle of summer, why not stop right now and listen to some Christmas music? It might be a good time to fall on your knees.

6) Summarize in four or five sentences what you have learned from this chapter.

3

# Our Perfected Savior

*For it was fitting that he, for whom and by whom all things exist,*
*in bringing many sons to glory, should make the founder*
*of their salvation perfect through suffering.*

HEBREWS 2:10

As we realized in the last chapter, the founder of our salvation, Jesus Christ, the one who would bring us as adopted sons to glory, *had to be made perfect through suffering.* Does that statement baffle you? It should; but perhaps we can gain a bit more understanding if we stop to contemplate it for a while. How is it that the founder of our salvation needed to be made perfect? Wasn't Jesus already perfect? How would suffering make him any better than he already was?

The exquisite mystery, endless delight, and comfort found in these words could fascinate our finite minds for our entire lives. Why would the Son of God willingly condescend to be made "perfect through suffering"? How could that happen? It is to this facet of his incarnation that we turn our attention now, and though we'll just scratch the surface, I trust that these thoughts will encourage and comfort you.

## PERFECTED IN OBSCURITY

When we consider Jesus's work on our behalf, we usually think it began with his baptism in the Jordan when he was about thirty years old. And in one sense that is true, for his public ministry did begin there in those muddy waters in Palestine. But if we consider only the three-and-a-half years of his public ministry, if our understanding of his work pauses after a brief celebration at Bethlehem to resume only at his baptism in the Jordan, we rob ourselves of the comfort that his whole life of isolation, obscurity, and obedience are meant to bring us.

Jesus willingly hid himself away in Nazareth for thirty years. Generally ignored, he toiled without complaint, suffering humbly on our behalf. He lived as Jesus the child, big brother, carpenter, and single man providing for his family. He voluntarily adopted all these roles for us. His life as a young man with sawdust in his eyes, serving his widowed mother and siblings, was no meaningless placeholder while he counted the days until he could step onto the scene to do something really important. No, he wasn't merely treading water. He was living life for us, and he was being perfected through the suffering of life in a sin-cursed world. It was for us that he suffered, lived, and loved every day for thirty years. The one who didn't grasp after the equality with God that was rightfully his, "emptied himself" and became a servant (Phil. 2:6–7) and learned by experience what it was to be "gentle and lowly in heart" (Matt. 11:29) as he suffered in human frailty year after year.

## SATISFYING THE LAW'S DEMANDS

Why did Jesus have to live all those years in obscurity? For two simple reasons. First, *he needed to fulfill the law in our place.* Every single moment of every single day of his private life, even before his public ministry began, Jesus worked to fulfill the law for us. Why? Because throughout our lives we have failed to obey; we have left the law unfulfilled. Every day he was earning a righteousness for us, a righteousness that is summed up by perfect compliance to this law: "You shall love the Lord your God with all your heart and with all your soul and with all your mind and with all your strength and your neighbor as yourself" (Luke 10:27). What was he doing while he played in the dirt as a toddler? While he labored in the carpenter's shop as an apprentice? When he helped with dinner as a twenty-something? He was being perfected so that he could find you and make you one with him. He loved God and those around him *for your sake, in your place.* Everything that you've left undone, he did for you. Every sin you've committed, he joyfully shunned out of love for you. Day after day for thirty years his one desire was to please his Father and live perfectly in your place so that he could bring you to glory.

Jesus was so good that the righteousness of his daily life exceeded "that of the scribes and the Pharisees," and it had to be that way because it was our only hope of entering the kingdom of heaven (Matt. 5:20). Any obedience we might gin up (on a good day) could never compare to the outward submission and strict ritual those Pharisees practiced. And yet, Jesus's obedience exceeded even this. Jesus wasn't more outwardly religious than the Pharisees. He wasn't concerned about punctilious compliance to human tradition. Rather, he was utterly holy. His obedience was from the heart, in adoration and faith while suffering in obscurity, without standing on street corners showing off (Matt. 23:5) or seeking to garner glory from others (John 5:44). In the restating of God's law from that mount in Galilee, Jesus ratcheted up God's demands, revealing the law's true intent—inward holiness (Matt. 5:1–7:27), all the while knowing that his listeners wouldn't be able to fulfill it but knowing that he would in their place.

Jesus fully satisfied the righteousness that the law, which could never pass away until all had been fulfilled, demanded (Matt. 5:18). Since the garden of Eden, the law had demanded obedience and punished disobedience through the shedding of blood and death. But Jesus's life of ordinary (yet spectacular) obedience changed everything. Through his obedience he silenced the law's demands forever. And his shed blood and death, which would be unnecessary in his own case, would be offered later, not for his sins but for ours.

His daily obedience was sufficient to completely satiate this terrifying mandate: You "must be perfect, as your heavenly Father is perfect" (Matt. 5:48). Have you ever seriously considered the ramifications of that demand? Before the eyes of God, nothing less than perfection is required. Neither, "I did my best," nor, "I didn't know what I was supposed to do, but I tried," will suffice. Perfect obedience is required—oh, but don't despair! Perfection is what he has provided! It was *his* righteousness that exceeded that of the Pharisees, *his* obedience that was as perfect as his Father's.

But his obedience was no mere outward compliance. Jesus described his obedience as "always" doing the things that pleased his Father (John 8:29). Think on that for a moment. Every second of every day of his existence, his heart and mind and soul and strength orbited about this one desire: *Father, I want to please you because I love you and because I love my bride.* Always one desire only: to love. He lived a life of complete inward holiness and answered every demand of his Father's law.

## QUALIFIED TO DIE

Second, Jesus lived perfectly so that his death would result in our redemption, in our debt being fully discharged. Every day—when he loved those who hated him, when he served those who would spitefully use him, when he was patient with those who willfully misunderstood him, when he blessed and protected women who flirted with him—he kept himself spotless so that he would be qualified to die in our place. If he had sinned even once, then his death would not have benefited us in the least. His death would have been just like every other death: a just penalty for sins committed. But he didn't sin, no, not once, not ever, and it is this exquisite, boundless sinlessness that qualifies him to pay off *all* our liabilities before heaven's judgment seat. *This sinlessness qualified him to die sacrificially in our place.* Because of our daily sin, we've earned death. Because of his daily obedience, he earned life. But instead of life, he received the death we earned, and we receive the blessings he deserved. He was "holy, innocent, unstained, separated from sinners" (Heb. 7:26), and because of that holiness he has "perfected for all time those who are being sanctified" (10:14). Because of his holy life and sacrificial death, we "*have been* sanctified through the offering of the body of Jesus Christ once for all" (v. 10). Because of his life of suffering obedience, because of his suffering in death, if you believe in him, right now your righteousness exceeds that of the scribes and the Pharisees; right now you are perfect as your heavenly Father is perfect.

## INNOCENCE WAS NOT ENOUGH

At his birth Jesus was completely innocent like Adam had been in the garden of Eden. Yes, at creation Adam was innocent and sinless, but he was untried; he was innocent, but he wasn't yet holy. Adam was capable of sin and eventually fell. And in his fall, all of humanity's innocence was forever destroyed.

As the second Adam, Jesus was innocent, too, but untried innocence wouldn't have been sufficient for our salvation. He had to be perfected through suffering. He needed to accomplish more than a death in untried innocence would accomplish, or else an assassination by Herod at Jesus's birth would have been sufficient for our salvation. No, he needed to live a full life of joyous obedience in order to save us. Innocence wasn't enough; in order to accomplish his mission he had to be holy. He grew from *blissful innocence to tested holiness* in the crucible of daily life. He suffered in all the ways you are suffering today, and yet his suffering was not a result of his sin—it was a suffering for yours.

> It was through this course of obedience and of learning obedience that he was made perfect as Savior, that is to say, became fully equipped so as to be constituted a perfect Savior. . . . And this is just saying that it was the obedience learned and rendered through the whole course of humiliation that made him perfect as the captain of salvation. It is obedience learned through suffering, perfected through suffering, and consummated in the suffering of death upon the cross that defines his work and accomplishment as the author of salvation.[1]

63

## OBEDIENCE IN WEAKNESS

Jesus learned how to obey with only the limited strength he possessed as a human. He was the Word become flesh (John 1:14). True flesh, true weakness, just like yours. He was not "the Word become sort of like you," or "the Word like you on the outside but deity on the inside," but actually just like you. In his humanity he would know by experience that we "are dust," for personally, again by experience, he "knows our frame" (Ps. 103:14). It was necessary that he learn by experience what obedience was like for the weak, so he obeyed for you, in your weak flesh.

He learned obedience by what he suffered, and this suffering included being weak, finite, and limited like you. He wasn't omniscient. He didn't know everything there was to know. He wasn't omnipresent, nor did he use his power as God to shelter himself from suffering. He was limited in all the ways you are limited—in strength, understanding, wisdom, and faith. *Like you, he had to walk by faith rather than by sight.* Jesus didn't have special vision that enabled him to see invisible realities. No, when he looked at the sky, he saw just what you see: sky, clouds, sun. Just like you, he had to believe the Word (and the Word he had consisted only of the Old Testament scriptures). Like you, he had to trust that his Father would accomplish all his will through him at the right time without having the surety that seeing into the future would have given him. Trust was an act of faith for him just as it is for you, yet he never doubted that his Father's word was true. Think of that. Because he lived in perfect faith for you, that's your record today. He lived the life of the faithful Jewish son; he died the death of an unfaithful, unbelieving infidel—for you, so that you might be found in him.

## HIS BAPTISM FOR THE REMISSION OF OUR SINS

Jesus's first public act was to travel from Nazareth to the Jordan River to be baptized by his cousin. John had appeared on the scene before him, preaching a baptism of repentance for the forgiveness of sins. Having been questioned by the religious leaders about his ministry, John testified that "among" them there stood one they did not know who would baptize with the Holy Spirit (John 1:26). It was to prepare the way for Jesus that John was baptizing the repentant and warning the unrepentant of coming judgment. But he testified, in fulfillment of Isaiah 40:3, that he was merely the "voice of one crying out in the wilderness," preparing the way "for the Lord God of the Old Testament (Yahweh himself) to come to his people through the wilderness."[2] In one sense, John was his cousin's public relations firm, doing business in the wilderness and in exile.

You can understand, then, why when Jesus approached John and asked John to baptize him, everything within John recoiled at the request. He couldn't understand why the sinless one should be baptized by him, a sinner. So initially John refused; "I have need to be baptized by you, not you by me," he objected. And here we see that even though John was a great prophet, not even he understood the lengths to which the Lord would go to save and retrieve his people. You see, although John knew that Jesus was indeed one *among* us, he didn't yet know the extent to which this Holy Son of God was one *of* us.

Still, Jesus insisted that John baptize him in order "to fulfill all righteousness" (Matt. 3:15). So John consented. What on earth was Jesus doing there in those muddy waters? He had no need to repent, to wash away sins, or make a public declaration of his faith. What was he doing? *He was being baptized in your place.* He was confessing your lack of love, your idolatry, your disobedience and unbelief. He was being righteous in your place, for you. "His submission to baptism was in a vicarious capacity, on behalf of his people, whom he was to save from their sins (Matt. 1:21)."[3]

Luke 3:21 tells us that Jesus wasn't silent while he was being baptized. No, he was praying. What did he pray? The Bible doesn't tell us, but we can be sure that he was submitting himself to the will of his Father and identifying himself as one of us. Was he confessing our sins? Again, the Bible doesn't say but we do know that he so completely identified with us that it isn't impossible to think it. In those wilderness waters he was our representative.

Have you been baptized? I hope so. But what if you aren't sure that you were completely sincere, completely believing? What if you had wrong motives or were baptized as a child just to make your parents happy? What if you were baptized as an infant and you're not sure whether that is sufficient? Do not fear. Jesus was baptized in your place, aware of and repenting for all your hypocrisy, ignorance, and unbelief, and his baptism is completely righteous and efficacious for you if you believe in him today.

## THE HEAVENS ARE FINALLY OPENED

Now, at last, we have arrived at the first instance since his miraculous birth in which we can see the direct intervention of God. We finally see what we would have expected to see all along: a loving Father hovering over a beloved Son. As I've said, Jesus's life was exactly like yours and mine until this point. He didn't get any special perks or supernatural privileges; like you he walked by faith, not by sight. But for a moment, at his baptism, heaven opened, and we see, along with him, the reality he believed long before he actually saw it. For when Jesus went up from the water, "the heavens were opened to him" (Matt. 3:16), and John saw the Spirit of God descending like a dove and coming to rest on him, signifying the pouring out of the anointing of the Holy Spirit. At that anointing Jesus is declared as the anointed one, the Christ, the long awaited Messiah. Now he is known not only as Jesus, the incarnate one, but as Jesus Christ, the anointed Messiah.

After pouring out the Spirit upon his Son, a proud Father from heaven launches his Son's ministry by declaring, "This is my beloved Son, with whom I am well pleased" (Matt. 3:17). Because Jesus had lived obediently through all those years in Nazareth, before the beginning of his ministry, before his greatest act of obedience on the cross, he had already earned the title "well-pleasing, beloved Son." For the first time, the heavens open to him, and the

Son heard the audible voice of the Father as the Holy Spirit filled him. How his great heart must have been near to bursting with joy after thirty years of silent obedience, of walking by faith alone.

John then declares Jesus's new name: "the Lamb of God, who takes away the sin of the world" (John 1:29). Jesus, the anointed one, the Christ, now has a new public identity. He is the Lamb without blemish, who will be slaughtered for the sins of his people. Jesus must come to us as not as a lion but as a lamb, the Passover lamb we must partake of or death will not pass us by.

## HIS TEMPTATION IN THE WILDERNESS

Jesus Christ's baptism in water and Spirit do not signal an easing of his trials or suffering. No, in fact, they were signs that his suffering would increase; now the time of severe trial for the founder of our salvation would commence. Immediately after his baptism Jesus was driven out into the wilderness, exiled by the Spirit to face the first of his great confrontations with our enemy. He went into the wilderness and temptation so that he would be further perfected through suffering.

Although Jesus had already learned obedience through suffering, his perfecting was not yet complete. Yes, he had suffered for a lifetime, for thirty years, and he had matured and settled into a life of faithful obedience. But now the stakes were higher and the temptations so much greater: he was about to have a one-on-one conflict with a spirit being, with his eternal enemy Satan. Neither you nor I have any idea what that sort of confrontation is like. Even if you have endured deep temptation, you have always done so under the protection of your Savior. We can't imagine what this trial was like for Jesus as he faced Satan not as another spirit being but as the Word made flesh. It was for this momentous conflict that the Father sent the Spirit upon the Son at his baptism. In this struggle, he would need the Spirit's strengthening as he faced Satan's malevolent temptations to unbelief and self-aggrandizement, and he resisted him by faith alone.

INCARNATION

Consider, too, what shape Jesus's body was in when he faced these temptations; he was, in essence, starving, dehydrated and suffering from exposure. He had gone without food and undoubtedly without good rest for forty days. He had lived in the wilderness, exposed to the elements, finding water where he might—baking under the blistering sun, freezing in the endless night, lying down on rocks and dirt, with only his cloak (dear cloak soon to be bartered away) for covering. And "he was with the wild animals" (Mark 1:13).

The setting for the temptation Adam endured was a beautiful garden filled with comfort, indescribable food, and the sweet fellowship of wife and Lord. In contrast, our Savior's temptation was in a wilderness; he was utterly alone, more isolated than we have ever been, with only faith in his Father's Word to sustain him.

## SATAN'S WARCRAFT

Let's take a few moments now to consider the temptations Jesus faced and remember that he faced them so that he, as a weak human standing in our place, could vanquish Satan and thereby undo his grip on us. Humanity had lived under the curse of death for sin since the fall and under the rule of the prince of the power of the air; Jesus Christ had to succeed exactly where we failed so that the curse for disobedience would be broken.

> Since therefore the children share in flesh and blood, he himself likewise partook of the same things, that through death he might destroy the one who has the power of death, that is, the devil. (Heb. 2:14)

Jesus "partook" of flesh and blood to destroy death and Satan's power in our lives.

### STONES TO BREAD

The first temptation Jesus faced was to make rocks into bread. Satan had conquered both Adam and the children of Israel by means of a temptation to eat sinfully. He undoubtedly felt confident that Jesus, who was starving to death at this point, would certainly use his power to satiate himself and show off his abilities. Obviously the Christ possessed the power to multiply bread and did so on two subsequent occasions. The question here was whether he would use his deity for self-promotion and self-gratification. He had refused this temptation for many years as he labored like any other carpenter, and because of his habitual obedience, he would refuse it again here.

How did he succeed in this battle? He believed his Father's Word, that true life does not flow from anything of this earth; it doesn't flow to those who seek to keep their lives but to those who seek to lose them in self-sacrificing faith, believing that God's Word is reliable. Jesus would bet his life on it. "It is written, 'Man shall not live by bread alone, but by every word that comes from the mouth of God'" (Matt. 4:4).

## IMPRESS US WITH A TRICK

Jesus's second temptation (in Matthew's Gospel) was to force God to perform a miracle, to draw attention to himself, and to force God to rescue his Son in a spectacular way.

> Then the devil took him to the holy city and set him on the pinnacle of the temple and said to him, "If you are the Son of God, throw yourself down, for it is written,
>
> 'He will command his angels concerning you,' and 'On their hands they will bear you up, lest you strike your foot against a stone.'" Jesus said to him, "Again it is written, 'You shall not put the Lord your God to the test.'" (Matt. 4:5–7)

Jesus knew that a time would undoubtedly come when he might hope for a spectacular deliverance, but this was not that time. Instead, he resisted the temptation to promote himself. He would not promote himself, nor would anyone else except a wild-looking man clothed in camel's hair who baptized in the wilderness. Jesus would refuse the temptation to advertise his deity as he repelled the world's wisdom and its path to "successful ministry."

## JUST A LITTLE HALLELUJAH WILL DO

Satan's final temptation of our Savior was to bow down and worship Satan so that he might receive "all the kingdoms of the world" (Luke 4:5). This is interesting because Jesus was already a king and would, in fact, rule over all the kingdoms of the world, but he wouldn't take the easy way; his pathway to exaltation was through the suffering of death, not idolatry. Think of the faith that must have been glowing red-hot when he commanded, "Be gone, Satan! For it is written, 'You shall worship the Lord your God and him only shall you serve'" (Matt. 4:10).

Again, the Lord Jesus had a practiced habit of exclusive worship of his Father. His worship and service throughout all those years in Nazareth enabled him to banish the Devil's enticements.

Idolatry, the worship of anything or anyone other than the true God, is, of course, the heart of every temptation we face. *Will you believe that God is as good as he says he is* or *will you wonder if there isn't something lacking in him?* Every temptation is a trial of our faith in God's promises. *Will we be satisfied with what he gives us and believe that he is loving and good, or will we look at everything the world has to offer and worship that?*

Jesus faced and answered every one of these temptations with verses from Deuteronomy. His quoting these specific passages is significant because it signified that his whole trial was as the new Son, the second Adam, the true Israel, the faithful Jew. He wandered in the desert for forty days as the Israelites had for forty years. As he wandered there, he refused all the temptations of the Enemy that those earlier had succumbed to. He refused to complain about food or go outside of God's will to get bread to provide for himself. He refused to try God as the Israelites had tried him in the wilderness. Paul wrote, "We must not put Christ to the test, as some of them did and were destroyed by serpents" (1 Cor. 10:9). He would not presume on God's goodness by forcing God to work on his behalf. And, unlike them, he refused to worship anyone other than his Father. No golden calf that just happened to appear out of the fire for him (Ex. 32:24). He obeyed through great suffering as the exiled second Adam.

"If he had called upon his divine powers to make the temptation easier for himself, then he would not have obeyed God fully *as a man*," and his obedience would not have sufficed for our salvation.[4] No, the law demanded that a man must obey, and it was as a man, with all the weakness and frailty you experience every day, that he obeyed. The temptation was to use his divine power to "cheat" a bit on the requirements and make obedience somewhat easier. But he resisted, for you, so that he could rescue you from your wilderness and death.

After Satan tried (and failed) at every temptation, after Jesus, this dear man who was weak and finite like us, had succeeded where we have failed, then (and only then), "the devil left him, and behold, angels came and were ministering to him" (Matt. 4:11).

## OUR DEFEATED FOE

Not only did Jesus obey in our place, but he also crushed the power of Satan in our place. Satan's power lies in his ability to tempt and accuse us. But Jesus utterly crushed him in the wilderness. That means that when Satan comes to tempt you and tell you that you need to grasp something outside of God's will for you, you can say, "No, I have everything I need in the Christ who defeated you out of love for me." When he seeks to push you into unbelief by accusing you of sin, you can say that while it is true you are a sinner, your brother Jesus Christ lived perfectly in your place, so you are no longer guilty before him. Remember, the only power that Satan has now is to roar like a vicious lion the law's demands in your conscience and accuse you of irredeemable failure. He has no other power over you but to insidiously slander God's faithful love in your ears. Because Jesus was successful in his temptations, when

Satan comes to accuse you (his name, Satan, means "accuser"), you don't need to try to defend yourself with your own record. All you have to do is recall the perfect obedience of the Son in your place and go on your way in faith.

### A Note on Impeccability

*Impeccability* is a word that means that one is free from sin. In considering Jesus's incarnation, people through the centuries have discussed whether Jesus could have sinned. Because the Bible teaches that the man Jesus was tempted in every way as we are, there has to be a possibility that in his humanity, Jesus could have sinned (although because he was God, he never would). This means that Jesus's temptations in his humanity were real temptations, not faux temptations; they felt like true temptations to him just as they feel to you. He was truly tempted in his human nature and could have sinned if he had chosen to do so. But Jesus is not merely a man; he is also God, and in his divine nature he would not give in to sin, because God "cannot be tempted with evil" (James 1:13). Remember, in order for Jesus to be our substitute, he had to experience everything that we do. He refused to rely on his divine nature to make resisting sin and obedience easier for him. He met every temptation not by his divine power but on the strength of his human nature.

And that is the crux of the matter. Jesus didn't use his deity to shelter himself from true temptation, and in this we can be so encouraged. When we face temptations of any sort, whether they are temptations to sin blatantly or simply to give in to doubt or unbelief, we can trust, knowing that Jesus knows what this feels like and has walked there before us.

## HIS PUBLIC MINISTRY

After returning victoriously from his battle in the wilderness, Jesus called disciples to himself and went into the synagogue.

> And the scroll of the prophet Isaiah was given to him. He unrolled the scroll and found the place where it was written, "The

Spirit of the Lord is upon me, because he has anointed me to proclaim good news to the poor. He has sent me to proclaim liberty to the captives and recovering of sight to the blind, to set at liberty those who are oppressed, to proclaim the year of the Lord's favor. . . . Today this Scripture has been fulfilled in your hearing." (Luke 4:17–19, 21)

After thirty years of silence and obscurity, after baptism and battle in the wilderness, Jesus the Christ blew open the doors and revealed his true identity. He is *the* servant, the long-awaited one, the Messiah, and the time for his public work on our behalf had begun.

Notice how he describes his ministry. He does not come as a life coach or a great example to follow. He comes as a preacher of good news to those who know they lack spiritual wealth. He is there to open prison cells to those in captivity to guilt and sin. He opens the eyes of those who know they are blind and leaves in darkness those who think they can see. And, finally, he liberates those oppressed by the law, sin, and death and proclaims over all his people: "You are favored by God! This is the time of my favor, my mercy, my grace! You are found, we are one!"

For the next three-and-a-half years, Jesus went throughout all Israel as the prophet (fulfilling Deuteronomy 18:15), teaching in their synagogues, and proclaiming the good news. He proved that the word he preached was truth by

healing every disease and every affliction among the people. So his fame spread throughout all Syria, and they brought him all the sick, those afflicted with various diseases and pains, those oppressed by demons, epileptics, and paralytics, and he healed them. (Matt. 4:23–24)

He had relationships with the lowliest of people; he looked into their hearts and pointed out their sin and yet flooded them with mercy and grace as his daily act of atonement even before his final act on the cross. The ill, the unwashed, and the poor pressed in on him from every side and wore him out. He let them touch him, and yet he continued to love and offer himself to them.

## OUR OBEDIENT BROTHER, REPRESENTATIVE, REDEEMER, HUSBAND

This is your Savior. He was the obedient one, the true man who bore our frailty and yet never gave in to the temptations he faced every day. He, himself, asked the question, "Which one of you convicts me of sin?" (John 8:46). Which one of us could imagine saying such a thing? Paul, who called himself "foremost" among sinners (1 Tim. 1:15), declared that the Father had "made him to be sin who knew no sin" (2 Cor. 5:21). We are the sinners. He is our sinless brother. And yet, he is our brother. But he is also the ideal human. In all his temptations, Jesus obeyed God in our place and as our representative. He succeeded where Adam failed, where the people of Israel failed, and where we have failed, so that "by the one man's obedience the many will be made righteous" (Rom. 5:19).

And, oh, the preciousness of this thought: in all these temptations our sinless Savior gained an ability to understand our plight *by experience*. The Bible teaches us that Jesus gained an ability to understand and help us in all that we face: "Because he himself has suffered when tempted, he is able to help those who are being tempted" (Heb. 2:18). Jesus knows what you are facing today. He understands temptation. He knows what it is like to walk by faith alone.

> For we do not have a high priest who is unable to sympathize with our weaknesses, but one who in every respect has been tempted as we are, yet without sin. (Heb. 4:15)

And because he lived our life and was victorious in all the places where we have failed, he can now help us in whatever we face. This has a practical application for us: in every situation in which we are struggling with temptation, we can reflect on the life of Christ and ask if there are not some similar situations he faced, and then we can "with confidence draw near to the throne of grace, that we may receive mercy and find grace to help in time of need" (Heb. 4:16).

> We may come with boldness before God. That is precisely what we find people doing during the three years of his ministry, taking refuge under the wings of Jesus, flying from their own fear and unworthiness to find refuge in his answer to God on their behalf, and so finding shelter from the fierce accuser in being yoked together with the obedience and perfect life of the Son of Man.[5]

And who are we, now that we have believed that he has lived such a life in our place? We are members of his family: his mother, his brother, his sister (Matt. 12:49–50). We are found in his family, part of his body, his closest relative, his bride; and not only that, but we are, by the Holy Spirit, united to him as he has been united to us. In this great life that was lived for us, there is enduring comfort, but our comforts are just beginning. We must still climb up Calvary's hill and see our dear brother-husband-kinsman-redeemer bloodied on the tree. But for now, remember: "He was, and is forever, one of us," and he has fulfilled his mission to rescue us and make us his.[6]

## FOUND IN HIM

1) "For it was fitting that he, for whom and by whom all things exist, in bringing many sons to glory, should make the founder of their salvation perfect through suffering" (Heb. 2:10). Respond.

2) What trials or temptations are you facing in your life today? Can you think of a time when Jesus suffered in a similar way? How does his suffering console you and give you faith to persevere?

3) Read Luke 4:17–19, 21. When you think of Jesus's ministry, how do you see him? Do you see him primarily as a liberator or as a rule giver? How would seeing him primarily as a liberator change the way you live?

4) Summarize in four or five sentences what you have learned in this chapter.

# 4

# God's Love for Sinners

*In this the love of God was made manifest among us,*
*that God sent his only Son into the world,*
*so that we might live through him.*

1 JOHN 4:9

In my prayer time today I said, "Thank you, Lord, that you love sinners." And even though I had just prayed those words, I was taken aback by what I had said. The holy God to whom I pray loves sinners. Again, think of it: God loves sinners. Let the mystery of that truth impact your soul.

God loves sinners. How do I know? Because Jesus Christ himself declared, "For God so loved the world, that he gave his only Son, that whoever believes in him should not perish but have eternal life" (John 3:16). If I may be so bold, please allow me to paraphrase his words in this way:

> My Father so loves sinners that he has given me, his only Son, to them so that I might perish in their place, and if they believe this truth about me, they will never perish for their sin but live eternally with me.

That's how much he loves sinners. God loves sinners. Oh, amazing, liberating truth! Sweet consoling truth above all others: God loves sinners!

But no sooner do I utter those words then I realize yet another shocking truth: I don't, at least not consistently, wholeheartedly, or unselfishly. Yes, God loves sinners but I don't. I hate suffering for the sins of others. I cry foul when I have to pay the penalty for another's folly. "Why should I have to suffer for his foolishness?" I wonder. "Why should I have to inconvenience myself or pay her debt? I'm not the one who made unwise choices! Why should I have to face unpleasant consequences for another's stupidity?"

God loves sinners, but I don't. When I begin to grasp how hard it is to love sinners, I begin to understand the enormity of what Jesus has done. He is the only sinless one; the only one who has the right to withhold acceptance and love from sinners, and yet he loves them. He lived and died as the God-man because he loves sinners; he even loves sinners who self-righteously despise other sinners. He's so different from us. He's so loving. Why, I can barely let a rude driver cut me off without honking my horn or shooting him a dirty look. Love sinners? Me? Hardly. Sometimes I don't even like them; but he never let the coldness or puniness of my heart stop him from loving me!

## JESUS AMONG HIS BROTHERS

In this chapter, we'll be looking at the last few weeks of Christ's earthly life, the time leading up to the crucifixion. We will walk with him as he ascends another mount to be transfigured and then sit with him as he is anointed at Bethany. We'll see him as he rides astride a young donkey accepting the praise of the masses as they hail him as their King with loud hosannas. Yes, he will welcome their praises of him as their king, even though he knows they'll soon cry, "Crucify him!" and, "We have no king but Caesar!" (John 19:15).

Up until now, we've been primarily contemplating the humanity of Christ, how Jesus was just like us, how he concealed his true glory and refrained from using his deity to make a name for himself or protect himself from the suffering we experience. And even though at this point he does begin to reveal something of his nature as God, his adoption of our life of weakness continues to the very end. His self-disclosure doesn't originate in a desire to make a name for himself; rather, it flows out of his love for sinners. We begin to see his glory now, but he is still found with us so that we might be found in him.

Let's look now at the third year of his ministry about six months before his crucifixion. During his first two years he performed many miracles: he turned water into wine; cast out demons; healed the blind, the lame, and the leprous. He fed huge crowds of people from practically nothing on two separate occasions and raised two people from death. What we have never seen him do, though, is show off or create a pillow and a comfy bed to lay his dear body on. No, the goal of each of his miracles was to manifest his glory so that we might believe and live (John 2:11).

Jesus's miracles were not chance occurrences; they were paired with astonishing lessons, lessons brought with authority (Mark 1:22). He declared that those who thought they had sight were actually blind; he spoke to them in parables purposely keeping many of them in the dark. His teaching wouldn't satisfy the superficially curious, coddle the comfortable, or bolster the scribes' and Pharisees' self-esteem. In fact, on numerous occasions it seemed as though his teaching was meant to offend and confuse them; he frequently performed his miracles as a way to goad them into hostile action against him. He had one mission: to die. Everything he said and did was to the end that he would be made the sacrifice, so that if his beloved lost sinners would believe, they would have eternal life.

## EYEWITNESSES OF HIS MAJESTY

The transfiguration marks a turning point in the disciples' understanding of Christ's ministry, for it is here that they began to see that he was more than a miracle-working man espousing unexpected teachings and rattling the religious hierarchy. He was more than a prophet, more than a good man. He is God incarnate. Remembering this event, Peter wrote that the disciples were "eye-witnesses of his majesty" (2 Pet. 1:16). Here is Luke's account:

> Now about eight days after these sayings he took with him Peter and John and James and went up on the mountain to pray. And as he was praying, the appearance of his face was altered, and his clothing became dazzling white. And behold, two men were talking with him, Moses and Elijah, who appeared in glory and spoke of his departure, which he was about to accomplish at Jerusalem. Now Peter and those who were with him were heavy with sleep, but when they became fully awake they saw his glory and the two men who stood with him. And as the men were parting from him, Peter said to Jesus, "Master, it is good that we are here. Let us make three tents, one for you and one for Moses and one for Elijah"—not knowing what he said. As he was saying these things, a cloud came and overshadowed them, and they were afraid as they entered the cloud. And a voice came out of the cloud, saying, "This is my Son, my Chosen One; listen to him!" And when the voice had spoken, Jesus was found alone. And they kept silent and told no one in those days anything of what they had seen. (Luke 9:28–36)

Jesus invited his three dearest friends, Peter, James, and John, to join him as he journeyed up a high mountain. Upon arriving there, he began to pray while his worn out friends slept. But their sleep would soon be interrupted, for as he prayed, the light that was "a light for the nations," so that God's "salvation may reach to the end of the earth" (Isa. 49:6), burst forth from his mortal body.

> In the transfiguration His face, even in the flesh . . . shone like the sun, that is, the flesh which came from Mary and from our human race was transfigured to heavenly glory, so that it acquired . . . the glory, honor, and perfection of the Godhead.[1]

The disciples saw the true light standing incarnate right before their very eyes (John 1:5, 9; 1 John 2:9; Rev. 1:16). Jesus's appearance was so altered that his clothing glowed as though the full light of day was radiating from his flesh and through his garments. He "temporally broke through the veil of His humanity and the disciples saw His preexistent glory."[2]

The disciples stood in awe of the glorious light emanating from Jesus, but that's not all that awed them, for there, standing on the mountain, were Moses and Elijah, redeemed sinners welcomed into the fellowship of the Son. These men represented the main two facets of Israel's religious practice: the Law and the Prophets. But there they were, in conversation with the Lord. They were discussing Jesus's return from his mission: his imminent death, his exodus from this world of sin, and his return back into glory. Moses and Elijah weren't concerned about Jesus's success here, as if that were ever in doubt. No, there was one question on their minds: his return to his heaven.

This unique event would signify a change in the belief systems of the disciples. Peter, James, and John needed to see who their friend really was. And they needed to hear again the voice of his Father booming from heaven, "This is my Son, my Chosen One; listen to him!" (Luke 9:35), so that they would understand that it was to Jesus (and not to Moses or Elijah) that they were to listen. The transfiguration was significant because the Law and the Prophets held so much sway in the disciples' religious identity that even though they had heard God's voice proclaiming Christ's preeminence from heaven, they still didn't understand. In fact, they would continue to misunderstand it until after the resurrection when, as we've seen, on the road to Emmaus the risen Christ would teach them again that he, not Moses or Elijah, was the subject of all the Old Testament scriptures (24:27, 32).

Being the Lord who loves sinners as he does, Jesus knew that his friends would need a foundation on which to stand against the difficulties and persecutions ahead. In the weeks to come they would be tempted to pride as they saw the masses sing Christ's praise; they would ask for permission to call fire down upon unbelieving Samaritans; they would fall into despair as they heard Jesus speak of his death; and confusion would fill their hearts as he spoke to them of the resurrection. Events during the next few months would try them more than they could imagine at this juncture. And most of all, everything they thought they knew about the place of Moses and Elijah in their religious practice would be upended.

## "LET'S BUILD A NEW CHURCH! I'LL BE IN CHARGE!"

As this event was drawing to a close, Peter misinterpreted what he saw and tried to insert himself into the story. He thought that the point of this event was to prove that Jesus was on a par with Moses and Elijah. *Oh, I get it*, he probably mused. *Jesus is as important as the Law and the Prophets, so now it's time for me to step in and start a new religion. We can take what is good from Moses and Elijah and combine it with the amazing work of Jesus!*

> "Lord, it is good that we are here," [he babbled]. "If you wish, I will make three tents here, one for you and one for Moses and one for Elijah." (Matt. 17:4)

Yes, Peter was just the sort of person who would have loved to found a new religion. He loved being the subject of all the verbs. But before he could finish his sentence, the Father interrupted him. Peter had it all wrong, and the Father wasn't going to let him get very far down the road of his own personal glory story before he stopped him midsentence:

> [Peter] was still speaking when, behold, a bright cloud overshadowed them, and a voice from the cloud said, "This is my beloved Son, with whom I am well pleased; listen to him." (Matt. 17:5)

Don't miss what's happening here. Peter is trying to combine worship of the Law and the Prophets with worship of the Christ, and if there was ever a time in recorded history when God thundered,

"Shut up!" from heaven, it was then. Don't miss the sequence of events: the Lord Jesus was transfigured; he spoke with Moses and Elijah about his return home; Peter decided to start a new religion, and then, while he was "still speaking," a "bright cloud overshadowed them," and a voice from that cloud declared that Jesus was not simply one good man among three but rather the unique Son who pleases the Father. "Listen to him!" This wasn't some gentle dove fluttering down to earth with hints from heaven. No, this was the King of glory arriving on the scene to thunder out the regulations of his kingdom: "Jesus is the beloved Son!" "He pleases Me!" "Stop your religion-creating-god-playing-glory-story-man-exalting babble and listen to him!" In case you're wondering what this event was like, there was an immediate response on the part of the disciples: "They fell on their faces and were terrified" (Matt. 17:6). They knew they had just been disciplined, and when God disciplines someone from the midst of a "'bright cloud," the reaction isn't, "I think I'll start a new religion now." The reaction is terror.

But notice now the response of the Son: "Jesus came and touched them, saying, 'Rise, and have no fear'" (Matt. 17:7). Consider the voice of the Savior, who loves drowsy, babbling, ignorant, independent, fearful sinners. What does he have to say to you and me when we create our own gods, write our own glory stories, and babble on about our achievements? He touches us and says, "Rise, and have no fear." Yes, of course Jesus could have shown this glory of his at any time, but he didn't—because he wants us all to know that we can be near him and that he is just like us. Yes, he's preeminent, and his message and kingdom surpass both Moses and Elijah, but he's also our loving brother who does not want us to be terrified in his presence. "Rise," he whispers, "have no fear." As Charles Spurgeon writes, Jesus's conversation with the "pure spirits" of Moses and Elijah,

> did not make him disdain the touch of feeble flesh. Oh, the sweet comfort of that gentle touch! It aroused, consoled, and strengthened his amazed and trembling disciples. The touch of the man-

hood is more reassuring to poor flesh and blood than the blaze of the Godhead. The voice from heaven casts down; but the word from Jesus is, "*Arise*." The Father's voice made them sore afraid, but Jesus says, "*Be not afraid*." Glorious God, how much we bless thee for the Mediator![3]

After this amazing event, is it any wonder that John wrote, "The Word became flesh and dwelt among us, and we have seen his glory, glory as of the only Son from the Father, full of grace and truth" (John 1:14)? John had personally seen the glory of God resident in Jesus's human flesh—blazing glory, yes, but also a glory "full of grace and truth."

Later on, once Peter had been freed from his glory seeking, when he knew that martyrdom was upon him (2 Pet. 1:14), he referenced the transfiguration as the true teaching for which he would give his life:

> For we did not follow cleverly devised myths when we made known to you the power and coming of our Lord Jesus Christ, but we were eyewitnesses of his majesty. For when he received honor and glory from God the Father, and the voice was borne to him by the Majestic Glory . . . we were with him on the holy mountain. (2 Pet. 1:16–18)

Peter would never forget the transfiguration, but he still didn't understand that God's plan for his Son meant death, not earthly glory. And even though Jesus had corrected his disciples' expectations of fame and power, they still didn't understand. Before the transfiguration, Jesus warned them:

> The Son of Man must suffer many things and be rejected by the elders and chief priests and scribes, and be killed, and on the third day be raised. (Luke 9:22)

Then afterward he reiterated his warning in the strongest language:

> Let these words sink into your ears: The Son of Man is about to
> be delivered into the hands of men. (Luke 9:44)

Even though the disciples had been "eyewitnesses of his majesty," they were still completely blind about the true nature of Jesus's ministry. "Let these words sink into your ears," he told them. Why? Because they continued to misinterpret his mission. Yes, the glory of the transfiguration is remarkable, but we must never forget that humiliation and suffering, not mountaintop exaltation, awaited him on the road to our redemption.

There was one person who had some understanding of what awaited him, and although she didn't see the transfiguration, she knew the true nature of his mission, and she was ready to offer everything to him.

## A BEAUTIFUL THING

> Six days before the Passover, Jesus therefore came to Bethany,
> where Lazarus was, whom Jesus had raised from the dead. So
> they gave a dinner for him there. Martha served, and Lazarus was
> one of those reclining with him at table. Mary therefore took a
> pound of expensive ointment made from pure nard, and anointed
> the feet of Jesus and wiped his feet with her hair. The house was
> filled with the fragrance of the perfume. (John 12:1–3)

Here we are now in Bethany at dinner with some familiar faces: Simon, a leper who had been healed by Jesus; Lazarus, a man who had been dead for four days and yet lived; and Mary and Martha, Lazarus's sisters, who had been through Lazarus's death and had seen him respond to Christ's life-giving summons. With them are all the disciples, including Judas—greedy, faithless, pretend believer.

In the midst of this homey gathering, Mary's heart is overflowing. She's heard the news: the leaders are looking for Jesus to arrest him. Unlike his disciples, her ears have been opened to his warnings that he would be given over to the leaders who will kill him. She's heard her own heart's response: "I must comfort him; I must bless him; I must take one last opportunity to tell him how I love him," so she gathers up her courage and takes her most prized possession into trembling hands, and walking up behind him as he is reclining at a table, she breaks her gift, a flask of expensive oil, over his feet and wipes those feet with her hair.

This oil was no meager offering. In today's valuation, this vial of perfume would be worth about $43,000, an average yearly wage in America. Imagine walking into a room, taking a vial worth that much money, and pouring the contents of it onto the feet of one of the guests. I can imagine there would be great outrage at such wasteful extravagance—in fact, there was outrage then, too. But Jesus wasn't outraged by what Judas called "waste." He didn't look at her action as wasteful. He saw beauty in it. He saw what Mary had done and knew that her deed was glorious and that he was worth it.

Jesus knew that her gift was an act of love for him. He also knew that one week later, he would be dead. So he received her love and enjoyed the splendor of the fragrance and the relief that the oils brought to his dear feet, feet that would soon be bloodied. He also knew that she would be unable to properly anoint his body for burial once he was dead, for there would be no time for that once he was placed in the cold sepulcher. "She has done a beautiful thing to me. . . . She has done what she could; she has anointed my body beforehand for burial" (Mark 14:6–8).

Notice, if you will, how Jesus loves sinners. He actually enjoyed the way her hands felt on his feet as she wiped them with her hair. He welcomed her holy caresses and elevated her care of him to something more than she could ever have known: a gift for his death, a testimony to the splendor of his life. Let us think of what she did and of the great love she must have experienced to cause her to do such a thing for him. He looked at her, his sister, his bride. He pierced beyond her outward beautiful action and knew all her sin. He saw every mixture of faith and doubt in her heart and yet he enjoyed being comforted by her hands; but his enjoyment of her was never twisted into lust. It was holy love. Oh, the mercy and condescension of our Christ! How Jesus loves sinners! He loves their touch. He loves their worship. He loved Peter when he tried to start a new religion; he loves them even when they sin. He loved Mary when she anointed his body for burial. He loves sinners; he loves his bride.

Shortly after his anointing for burial, we finally see what so many had expected to see for years: his triumphant entry into the capitol city of his homeland.

## BLESSED IS THE KING WHO COMES IN THE NAME OF THE LORD

As a nation, the Israelites had been under the heel of Rome for over one hundred years. Even from before their bondage to Rome, the Jewish nation had been ruled by Babylon, Assyria, and Egypt. It had been nearly a thousand years since the golden age of King David and his son King Solomon. Jerusalem had not seen a Jewish monarch riding into her gates in a millennium, but she was about to—just not the sort of king she expected.

Like every other oppressed nation, Israel had been looking for a deliverer. During the time of the judges, the nation had begun to hope for a human king, for a man who could rescue them and give them the security they thought the other nations around them had. So they asked Samuel the priest to anoint a king for them and even though he warned them that a king would undoubtedly break God's command by multiplying horses, riches, and wives (Deut. 17:14–20), they insisted. So Samuel anointed Saul, but through his unbelief Saul lost his kingdom, and David took his throne. After David, his son Solomon reigned, and, as Samuel foretold, Solomon broke every single one of God's laws for kings.

The Israelites of Jesus's day looked back on the monarchy of David and Solomon and longed for their return. They longed for the days when their nation had a king they could be proud of, a king who would protect them from and rid them of their despised overlords, a king who would provide for them so that the crushing poverty and humiliation of being part of a pagan empire would be vanquished. They longed for a king like Solomon—proud, rich, someone you could tie your identity to. They would have been happy to welcome Solomon into their city, because Solomon was a king you could be proud of. After all, he had fourteen hundred chariots which were

> maintained largely for the sake of pomp and display. In one year . . . the gold revenues of Solomon weighed 666 talents (25 tons). . . . Seven hundred of Solomon's wives were princesses, i.e., members of the royal houses of neighboring nations. His concubines—wives of secondary rank—numbered three hundred.[4]

Yes, Solomon was a king you could brag about. He had wealth, women, and military might. He was just the sort of ruler that glory-hungry people wanted to welcome. But Israel's true King was different. Here is Matthew's description of Jesus's coronation procession—notice the difference between this King and Solomon:

> Now when they drew near to Jerusalem and came to Bethphage, to the Mount of Olives, then Jesus sent two disciples, saying to them, "Go into the village in front of you, and immediately you will find a donkey tied, and a colt with her. Untie them and bring them to me. If anyone says anything to you, you shall say, 'The Lord needs them,' and he will send them at once." This took place to fulfill what was spoken by the prophet, saying, "Say to the daughter of Zion, 'Behold, your king is coming to you, humble, and mounted on a donkey, on a colt, the foal of a beast of burden.'"
>
> The disciples went and did as Jesus had directed them. They brought the donkey and the colt and put on them their cloaks, and he sat on them. Most of the crowd spread their cloaks on the road, and others cut branches from the trees and spread them on the road. And the crowds that went before him and that followed him were shouting, "Hosanna to the Son of David! Blessed is he who comes in the name of the Lord! Hosanna in the highest!"

And when he entered Jerusalem, the whole city was stirred up, saying, "Who is this?" And the crowds said, "This is the prophet Jesus, from Nazareth of Galilee." (Matt. 21:1–11)

Think about the differences between the king the Israelites wanted and the King God had given them. Solomon could claim David for his father; Jesus had been thought of as a bastard child. Solomon was born in a king's palace and never knew a single day of poverty or suffering; Jesus came from a rustic village. Solomon was the richest man of his day—a real Bill Gates or Donald Trump; Jesus didn't own a donkey nor did he have a place to lay his head (Matt. 8:20). Solomon had allied himself through marriage with all the powerful people of his day; Jesus was a single man, surrounded by fishermen, tax gatherers, and women, many of whom had a checkered past. Solomon had carte blanche. He could do whatever he wanted, whenever he wanted. He ruled over Israel during a time of peace and never had to go to war. His kingdom was never divided. Conversely, although Jesus had the power to do anything he wanted, he had humbled himself and taken on the form of a servant. He could have called down angels to assist and comfort him, but he refused and instead chose to embrace our life of suffering. In the eyes of the world, Solomon had everything going for him. He was a great king. Jesus was a poor nobody. But that's not how Jesus saw it. When speaking of himself he said, "Something greater than Solomon is here" (Matt. 12:42). The things we esteem and the things God values are completely at odds, aren't they?

Up until this time, Jesus had entered cities without any pomp. He had frequently told people not to report that he had healed them. He hadn't even let demons proclaim his true identity. He had warned the disciples not to talk about the transfiguration until after his resurrection, and he had solemnly charged Peter not to repeat the fact that he was the Christ.[5] And now, even in this event, even in his triumphal entry into Jerusalem, he still is shunning the majesty that usually accompanies great authority and power. Yes, he is allowing himself to be hailed as the "Lord who saves" (to fulfill Scripture), but he does not do so from a great golden chariot, surrounded by all the trappings of great wealth. He does so from a borrowed donkey because he is humble and will not give in to the temptation to try to impress the city with his power. His life is a repeating statement of humility. He doesn't put on airs.

Do you want to know what Jesus is like? He rides into his capitol city as king on a borrowed donkey, and he does so because he loves sinners. He continually humbles himself so that we might feel as though we can come to him. If we saw him in all his heavenly majesty, we would cringe in fear. But fearful groveling is not what he wants from us. No, he would not take that form upon himself, so even in this, his hour of triumph, even when it seems as though the city had finally recognized her king (and even when we see him in heaven), he is still found in humble form, as a lamb slain. He knows our propensity to worship worldly power and success. He also knows that our power hunger and hero worship can breed a cringing fear and a pervasive distrust of him. He doesn't want us to be afraid of him. No, instead, Jesus comes to us as a man, in essence saying,

> I'm just like you. Yes, I am a king, but this is what kind of king I am: a humble, lowly servant, coming to bring you a salvation that is not what you expect, a salvation of your souls. I have chosen to be like you and suffer with you because I love you.

That's not to say that he doesn't continually prove that he is God or that he has power to command whatever he wills to occur. Does he need a donkey? All he has to do is say, "The Lord has need of it," and whatever he needs will be given to him. Of course, he could have sent the disciples anywhere, even to a Roman garrison, and by a miracle commanded that a horse and chariot with all of Rome's pomp be given him. But that's not what he does. No, instead he sends his disciples into a town close by where they will find a donkey and her little colt tied together. He doesn't demand that the owner give it to him though he has the right to. Instead he simply says, "The Lord has need of it," and the colt and his mother are given.

Notice also that he doesn't cover the young colt with all sorts of beautiful fabrics. No, instead his disciples and followers put their cloaks on it so that Jesus will have some comfort. He's so gentle that he won't even separate the little colt from his mother.

He's used to walking into cities and towns quietly, but this entry is different. He knows what will happen; he perceives the import of riding into town on a donkey. This was not the normal manner in which kings arrived, for they usually came as conquerors riding on horses. He's riding into Jerusalem on a colt, a symbol of peace, just as Solomon had ridden into Jerusalem at his coronation (1 Kings 1:38–40).

Jesus is, as always, very aware of the significance of what he's doing. He knows that he's fulfilling specific Old Testament prophecies:

> Rejoice greatly, O daughter of Zion!
>> Shout aloud, O daughter of Jerusalem!
> Behold, your king is coming to you;
>> righteous and having salvation is he,
> humble and mounted on a donkey,
>> on a colt, the foal of a donkey. (Zech. 9:9)

> Save us, we pray, O Lord!
>> O Lord, we pray, give us success!
> Blessed is he who comes in the name of the Lord!
>> We bless you from the house of the Lord. (Ps. 118:25–26)

And when the people pick up their palm branches and shout, "Hosanna," he knows that they are asking that he save them, and he also knows that is what he is about to do. But he won't do it the way they expect him to. He won't conquer their Roman overlords; no, he'll win thousands of them through love—in fact Rome herself will eventually become a center of Christianity. But before that happens, he knows that his bride's prayers for deliverance and shouts of allegiance will soon be turned to demands for his death, and he knows that death is the way he will answer her prayer for salvation.

He knows very well how the religious authorities, those who didn't know that he is greater than Moses or Elijah, will respond. Their indignation would be stoked hotter and hotter as they hear the riffraff shouting, "Hosanna! Save us!" And then, when they counseled him to silence the cries of the masses, he said that if they were quiet, the very rocks would worship him! And just to make sure they would take action against him immediately, he drove the crooks and religious hypocrites out of the temple.

On several other occasions, Jesus's followers had tried to crown him king by force (John 6:15). But now, on this one occasion, he allowed them to set him on the foal that was to carry him into the city. He knew that this was his time. This was the hour for his public coronation, a coronation that began in Bethlehem when kings from the east brought him gifts and anointing oils, that continued when the immoral woman in Luke 7 kissed his feet and washed them with her tears, and that continued to Mary's anointing of him at Simon the Leper's house. He was the King, and now it was time for the people to know it. He had been anointed by the Holy Spirit at his baptism, and he had said that he had been anointed to proclaim liberty to the captives, and now he wanted everyone to see him for who he was.

> In this one instance, he received worship. In their shouts the people were proclaiming Jesus as the Messiah and he let them do it. "Hosanna" means "Save, we pray thee." They repeat words from the *Hallel* (Psa. 148:1) and one recalls the song of the angelic host when Jesus was born (Luke 2:14). "Hosanna in the highest" (heaven) as well as here on earth.[6]

## WHO IS THIS?

"Who is this?" the people in Jerusalem asked. And that is a good question for us to consider. "Who is this?" This is Jesus, the prophet from Nazareth of Galilee. This is Jesus, the God-man who became a human being in order to be found with us. He is the man, the representative of our entire race of men and women who have failed to live in love and have needed but refused the salvation he has come to give. "Who is this?" He is the man whom children love to worship and whom disciples habitually misunderstand. He is the man who receives kisses and anointing oil, and then he rides calmly, lovingly, and gently to his death. "Who is this?" Jesus, the God-man, born in Bethlehem, lately of Nazareth. "Who is this?" He is the one who saves those whose hearts are so fickle that one day they proclaim him king and the next they call for his blood. "Who is this?" He is our king, our husband, our redeemer, our salvation. Hosanna! Blessed is he who comes in the name of the Lord to bring beloved sinners to life.

## FOUND IN HIM

1) Of the three vignettes presented in this chapter, which one(s) spoke most deeply to you? In which one do you see a personal propensity to fail to recognize Christ's work for you?

2) In what ways do you see yourself in the place of Peter, trying to establish a kingdom or religion of your own?

3) In what ways do you see yourself as Mary, worshiping her Savior against popular wisdom?

4) In what ways do you see yourself as the masses in Jerusalem— worshiping and crying out for salvation one day, refusing him and crying out for his death the next?

5) Summarize what you've learned in this chapter.

5

# O Sacred Head, Now Wounded

*Now before the Feast of the Passover, when Jesus knew that his*
*hour had come to depart out of this world to the Father, having*
*loved his own who were in the world, he loved them to the end.*

JOHN 13:1

It isn't an exaggeration to say that the point of Jesus's entire existence is now upon us. Jesus did not come to earth to be our example. He did not come to be our life coach, psychologist, mentor, or cheerleader. He came to be our redeemer and to bear all the weight of the wrath we deserve. He came to die, and in so doing, to glorify his Father by standing with us. The events we will consider now begin the finale of the drama begun in the heart of God before the foundation of the world. God would persist in loving his creation, and this love would bring death to him.

We're entering the Most Holy Place. This ground we're treading upon now is more sacred than any other—more sacred than Eden, Mount Sinai, or Bethlehem. This ground, which began to exist on the day when he commanded: "Let the dry land appear" (Gen. 1:9), would now be dampened by the tears of the man who writhes alone on it in agony. In a few short hours it would soak up that most precious fluid: blood and water from his pores, from his side. His blood was just like ours. It poured from his open wounds;

it coagulated in vain effort to try to staunch its flow. It smelled and tasted like your blood, and when it dripped into his eyes or down his back or off his feet there was enough of it to form a pool beneath him that reflected to heaven his marred visage. This muddy pool seemed to shout that his life was a cosmic hoax and that humble, pure love will always get its comeuppance. From this moment on, the sarcastic mantra of the hopeless human race will be, "No good deed goes unpunished."

Take off your shoes now and walk with me a while; take off all your self-protection, self-righteousness, hollow pride, excuse making, self-pity, and crass unbelief and walk humbly before your God. Lower your eyes, beat your breast, take off all you trust in, all you seek to impress with, all that assures you of your worthiness, and watch. Watch as he suffers more than any other person who has ever suffered. Humble yourself before this untold carnage.

## HIS THOUGHTS ARE NOT OUR THOUGHTS

Let us seek to pierce into the depth of this man's heart and mind. What occupied his thoughts as he began his journey up the holy mountain to his death? By the Spirit, John gives us insight into the thoughts that occupied the God-man's heart. What was he thinking of during his last few hours? We can begin to understand his thoughts by looking at John's description of them in the upper room:

> Now before the Feast of the Passover, when Jesus knew that his hour had come to depart out of this world to the Father, having loved his own who were in the world, he loved them to the end. . . . Jesus, knowing that the Father had given all things into his hands, and that he had come from God and was going back to God, rose from supper. (John 13:1, 3–4).

What was it that he thought of? Jesus certainly knew that his death was imminent, for he had spoken about it on many occasions. Just as he had known in his preexistent state that the time had come for him to enter into this world, he now knew it was time to depart and return home. This homecoming was a source of great joy to him (John 14:28) because he was returning to his Father. But notice, if you will, that the joy he felt at returning home didn't diminish his love for the people who had been given to him. The abundant joy he felt knowing that he was returning to his Father was tempered in his great heart by concern for his dear friends.

Toward them his disposition was this: "He loved them to the end." Think of that. He knew that soon they would leave him. Some would desert, one would deny, one would betray, but none would stand with him in his hour of trial. He knew all this about their weakness, yet he loved them to the end.

So what does he do? Does he set off flares at his great good fortune in returning home? Does he scold his disciples for their ignorance and selfish ambition? No, he humbles himself and washes their feet; he spends hours in discourse with them, telling them the truths they needed to hear; he initiates his Supper, feeding their souls with his body and blood; and he prays for them. Jesus spent his last few hours with his friends loving them and giving them all they would need. He loved them to the end.

Even when he faced Judas's betrayal, he still loved. John writes that he was "troubled in his spirit" (John 13:21) as he testified of Judas's treachery and fall. So far from wanting revenge or to shame his fatally flawed friend, Jesus is even distressed over having to tell his disciples who it is that will betray him. Who has ever loved like this man?

Let us leave the upper room now. We've seen enough of Peter, the self-made man who initially refused to have his feet washed and who then demanded a bath; we've heard enough of his, "Lord, I am ready to go with you both to prison and to death" (Luke 22:33), and of each of the disciples' similar protestations (Matt. 26:35). We've witnessed their selfish ambition as they jockeyed for position. And we've seen the Savior give bread to the betrayer who had gone out from the group. "And it was night" (John 13:30).

INCARNATION

## IN A GARDEN—AGAIN

Up now we tread to the garden of Gethsemane—another garden, another test, another Adam who will answer the same question we have all responded to since Eden. All of our salvation, every bit of our ransomed life, hangs in the balance as we listen carefully for his answer. Will this Adam trust? Will he obey? Or will we be consigned to spend an eternity in hell and isolation from all that is light and love?

The little group enters the garden, and he calls his three friends to walk farther in with him. Notice his attitude:

> He began to be sorrowful and troubled. Then he said to them, "My soul is very sorrowful, even to death; remain here, and watch with me." And going a little farther he fell on his face and prayed, saying, "My Father, if it be possible, let this cup pass from me; nevertheless, not as I will, but as you will." And he came to the disciples and found them sleeping. And he said to Peter [who had been so self-assured], "So, could you not watch with me one hour? Watch and pray that you may not enter into temptation. The spirit indeed is willing, but the flesh is weak." Again, for the second time, he went away and prayed, "My Father, if this cannot pass unless I drink it, your will be done." And again he came and found them sleeping, for their eyes were heavy. So, leaving them again, he went away and prayed for the third time, saying the same words again. (Matt. 26:37–44)

In the history of the world, no one has ever faced a trial like this. This trial would demand that Jesus humbly relinquish all that he was in himself: pure, innocent, unstained. He would become sin for us (2 Cor. 5:21); the blessed one would become a "curse" for us (Gal. 3:13); he would be "delivered up for our trespasses" (Rom. 4:25). He knew that soon he would be aware of all the sins that his beloved had ever committed against him while she committed the most grievous sin of all: killing the Son of God. He would stand before his Father, the Father around whom his entire life revolved, no longer clothed in his own righteousness but dressed in our filth, and his Father would turn in wrath from him. He would experience our exile. "Oh, my Father, why?" he would soon cry.

Why did Jesus tremble as he did in this garden? Was he afraid of the lash, the thorns, the spike, the spear, the cross? No! Ten thousand times, no! Mankind's most ingenious instruments of suffering were nothing compared to the just wrath of the Father, which he would soon experience. In a few short hours he would receive in his person and bear up under the full weight of all his Father's fury that would have been poured out on all of his people's souls for all of eternity. No one but God could bear up under this crushing weight. No wonder he fell on the ground and wept as he did.

Imagine, if you will, all of heaven watching the beloved Son in agony on the ground. How the holy angels must have wondered at this scene and then glanced back at the Father, hoping for the signal to go to the one they loved. At last one angel (only one?) was sent to strengthen him, and yet he continued to travail. "And being in an agony he prayed more earnestly; and his sweat became like great drops of blood falling down to the ground" (Luke 22:44).

Several times he went to his friends. He needed the comfort and strength that their companionship could give him; he longed to experience their care once again. And yet they slept because they were sad (Luke 22:45), and, like the rest of us, they hid from their sorrows under the cover of sleep. While he faced his sorrows alone, they slumbered. This dear man, this best of all humans, this loving, faithful friend, this pure and innocent husband, labored while his bride curled up under a cloak and protected herself from sorrow.

His prayers warred against all that he loved in his life and against all that in his humanity he treasured. "Will you trust?" "Will you obey, no matter that obedience means a complete denial of all that you cherish?" His life of obedience and even the temptation in the wilderness was child's play compared to this. He wasn't warring against Satan in that garden; no, he was warring against himself and all that he was in his humanity and his deity.

How does this trial end? Oh, thank God—with the Son's submission: "Abba, Father, all things are possible for you. Remove this cup from me. Yet not what I will, but what you will" (Mark 14:36). In filial humility, the Son addresses the Father in the most intimate of terms. "Abba," "Dada." As a toddler he had first mouthed that appellation when he looked at his earthly daddy; little lips forming two short syllables of love. Soon he had learned who his true Abba was, and it was to this Abba that he prayed in faith as he wept now. He was sorrowful to the point of death (Matt. 26:38), yet he never accused or doubted. "Abba, you can do anything. There is nothing impossible for you," he pled. "Let this cup pass." But it would not pass, so the man Christ Jesus rose from this battleground, already bloody, already exhausted, and, as a lamb being led to the slaughter, he willingly walked out to face his sleeping disciples, his betrayer, and the henchmen sent on a midnight errand from the temple erected to worship his Father. Night and the power of darkness was theirs, but this war was already over, and our rescuer had already stood in our place and passed this test in the garden where we had failed.

So he comes to sleepy disciples once more and tells them to rise. Rise my friends. Rise from your sleepy dreams of grandeur and your troubled nightmares of loss. Rise from your unbelief and from your guilty knowledge of your continual failure. Rise out of your doomed lineage and exiled wandering and stand with me. I am the new man. I have won. I will stand. I will be your captain, your representative, your head, your husband. Rise and know that the battle has already been won because I have determined to obey. I will stand before the danger. I will protect you. I will obey.

What was our part in this victory? What did we supply? It was won for us while we slept. The war had been won by a man who in every way represented us and would not take the easy road or renege or doubt or please himself. He saw the Father's hand rising to strike him, the shepherd, and still he cared for his flock (see Matt. 26:31). We sleep and dream and comfort ourselves. He stood obedient and faithful for us. Everything has already been settled. He has set his face like a flint, and now it is up to him to suffer. We are found; he is with us.

## BEFORE THE TRIBUNALS

Let us join him now before Caiaphas and the council. His friends have all left him—even Peter, who is warming himself by a fire nearby, has left him in his heart. "I do not know the man!" he swears (Matt. 26:72). But our kinsman-redeemer stands quietly before his accusers until the high priest demands, "I adjure you by the living God, tell us if you are the Christ, the Son of God" (v. 63). And finally he declares the truth that he knows will force their hand. Even then, he could have saved himself. Even then, he didn't have to make things so plain. But he has already fought that fight, so he speaks the words of his own execution, "You have said so" (v. 64). The high priest tears his robes. "What is your judgment?" he asks the crowd. "He deserves death" they cry (v. 66).

If ever there was a man who did not deserve death, it was this man. We deserve death. We have, each of us, earned the curse of death, which our disobedience has wrought. We should be standing there before this tribunal. Yet there he is—humbly, quietly, willingly—our husband, standing as a lamb ready to be slaughtered. "Then they spit in his face and struck him. And some slapped him, saying, 'Prophesy to us, you Christ! Who is it that struck you?'" (Matt. 26:67–68). Oh, the gentle humility of the Word made flesh, who with one glance could have obliterated these fools. But he did not come into the world to obliterate fools, but rather he came that this world of fools might be saved though him.

Because the Jews did not have the prerogative to commit a prisoner to execution, they had to use Rome's emissary, Pilate. So in the morning the religious leaders bound Jesus and led him away (why did they think they needed to bind him?) to Pilate. Quietly he goes; in humble obedience he places one foot in front of the other. He didn't use the strength he possessed as God to give him the ability to walk this road; he was exhausted. He hadn't slept since the night before. And still on he walked as a man.

He stood before Pilate, who asked him, "Are you the King of the Jews?" Once again, he knowingly says what will seal his fate: "You have said so" (Matt. 27:11). It is not his purpose to defend himself. It is his purpose to die, so he says only what will bring about that outcome. Being the spineless weasel that he is, Pilate doesn't want to bear the ultimate responsibility for sending a man he knows to be innocent to his death, so he sends him over to Herod, making a pretense of concerns about jurisdiction. Herod is happy to receive Jesus, but only because he wants to see him perform some magic (there's nothing like some nice Jewish party favors), and when Jesus refuses to perform, Herod sends him back to Pilate. Then, after a few more feeble attempts to release him, "[Pilate] took water and washed his hands before the crowd, saying, 'I am innocent of this man's blood; see to it yourselves.' And all the people answered, 'His blood be on us and on our children!'" (vv. 24–25). Yes, we agree: let his blood be on us and on our children.

## AMUSEMENT FOR BORED SOLDIERS

Pilate had Jesus scourged and then turned him over to the soldiers for crucifixion. But they didn't want to hurry to get to a boring crucifixion just yet, and, after all, *here we have a Jew dog who is claiming to be a king—what a great opportunity for every anti-Semite to get his licks in. Stupid Jews! Self-righteous swine!* What a great opportunity for every foot soldier who had cursed the emperor under his breath to pretend he was hitting his king. *We get to strip and mock and beat a king! And he's a Jew! What great fun! The stars must be aligned in our favor today!* So the soldiers threw down their dice and their other amusements, and a whole battalion of battle-hardened men, about six hundred of them, lined up to take their turn at making their friends laugh while our brother, our husband, suffered and bled. They looked at his naked body. They undoubtedly laughed at his circumcision. They found a scarlet robe and put it on him and gave him a pretend scepter. They knelt before him and mocked him, "Hail, King of the Jews!" (Matt. 27:29). They rolled on the ground laughing. This was the most fun they'd had since getting posted to this God-forsaken wasteland. Soon some clever man found a thornbush and twisted it into a crown that they forced into his sacred head. *Careful now, you don't want to get jabbed*, one friend spoke to another. When the merriment began to die down, when all the men were tired of making fun of this ridiculous Jew, those who enjoyed inflicting punishment took over, and they spit in his bloodied face and took his scepter reed and beat him on the head with it. But, a man's only got so much energy, and soon they decided that the party was over, so they "put his own clothes on him and led him away to crucify him" (v. 31).

## BEFORE THE HEAVENLY TRIBUNAL

Up Calvary's hill the man and the surrounding troops went. Finally his body gave way and he could no longer carry the crossbeam upon which he would be fastened. Simon of Cyrene was compelled to carry it to The Place of a Skull. As they laid him down on this most cruel instrument of torture and death, even Rome's executioners took pity and offered him wine mixed with gall— something of an anesthesia to dull the pain—but he refused it. It was his purpose to face all that the coming hours would bring without any pain dulled, any sense blurred. Spikes, bloodied from previous use, were hammered into his hands and feet. Pain shot up through his legs and across his shoulders as the cross was dropped rudely into the ground he had created.

Crucifixion, Rome's favorite mode of punishment, was not only a method of execution but also a method of humiliation. Normally the offender would be stripped naked and hung at eye level so that people could walk by and spit on the condemned criminal as he suffered. People were encouraged to taunt and mock those hanging there in agony. Rome had no compassion for her enemies: do what you like to an immobile traitor. Shame him.

Laugh at him. Enjoy yourself and learn what worldly powers do to any who refuse to bow before them.

How does the innocent one respond? Does he defend himself? Does he call down fire from heaven to consume his enemies? These are the first words he said as he hung between heaven and earth: "Father forgive them, for they know not what they do" (Luke 23:34). His concern as he suffers is that his Father would forgive. He listens to the pleas of the man next to him and promises him a life after this one: "Today you will be with me in Paradise" (v. 43).

His bruised and swollen eyes catch a glimpse of Mary his mother weeping in the crowd. Her heart has been pierced by many pains. She knows who he is; she knows what we've done to her Son, our brother. She's being upheld by his dearest friend, John, so in the midst of this unbelievable suffering Jesus speaks kindly to her, saying, "Behold your son!" and to John, who understood that her care would now fall to him, he said, "Behold your mother!" (John 19:26–27). He's still the single man providing for the needs of his household.

*And then the real suffering starts.*

The Father pours out all his wrath for all our sin on the Son and forsakes him! He sends him into exile for all our sin. "My God, my God, why have you forsaken me?" he cries (Matt. 27:46). The one who had said, "Yet I am not alone, for the Father is with me" (John 16:32) is now completely isolated. At the very moment when he should have been vindicated, when his obedience should have eventuated in his blessing, when the Father should have rescued him, he is deserted. Why?

As many were astonished at you—
> his appearance was so marred, beyond human semblance,
> and his form beyond that of the children of mankind—
so shall he sprinkle many nations;

kings shall shut their mouths because of him;
for that which has not been told them they see,
and that which they have not heard they understand.

Who has believed what he has heard from us?
And to whom has the arm of the LORD been revealed?
For he grew up before him like a young plant,
and like a root out of dry ground;
he had no form or majesty that we should look at him,
and no beauty that we should desire him.
He was despised and rejected by men;
a man of sorrows, and acquainted with grief;
and as one from whom men hide their faces
he was despised, and we esteemed him not.

*Surely he has borne our griefs*
*and carried our sorrows;*
*yet we esteemed him stricken,*
*smitten by God, and afflicted.*
*But he was pierced for our transgressions;*
*he was crushed for our iniquities;*
*upon him was the chastisement that brought us peace,*
*and with his wounds we are healed.*
All we like sheep have gone astray;
we have turned—every one—to his own way;
*and the LORD has laid on him*
*the iniquity of us all.*

He was oppressed, and he was afflicted,
yet he opened not his mouth;
like a lamb that is led to the slaughter,
and like a sheep that before its shearers is silent,
so he opened not his mouth.
By oppression and judgment he was taken away;
and as for his generation, who considered
that he was cut off out of the land of the living,
*stricken for the transgression of my people?*
And they made his grave with the wicked
and with a rich man in his death,

    although he had done no violence,
        and there was no deceit in his mouth.

*Yet it was the will of the* LORD *to crush him;*
    *he has put him to grief;*
when his soul makes an offering for guilt,
    he shall see his offspring; he shall prolong his days;
the will of the LORD shall prosper in his hand.
Out of the anguish of his soul he shall see and be satisfied;
    by his knowledge shall the righteous one, my servant,
    make many to be accounted righteous,
    and he shall bear their iniquities.
Therefore I will divide him a portion with the many,
    and he shall divide the spoil with the strong,
because he poured out his soul to death
    and was numbered with the transgressors;
yet he bore the sin of many,
    and makes intercession for the transgressors.
        (Isa. 52:14–53:12)

He suffered like this to bear your sin and make intercession for you, so that you would be accounted righteous, so that you could live and stop wandering.

Jesus Christ, the God-man, was tempted in every way as we are. He knows what it is like to walk by faith and not by sight—and he knows experientially what it is to look to a brazen heaven. He knows what it is to experience the guilt of sin and to continue to trust in his Father's grace, even though the weight of sin was crushing him. He knows what it is to deserve blessing and to receive a curse. He knows what God's wrath feels like and what it is for you and me when we just can't seem to find our way to God, when our sins have separated us from him, and when we're overwhelmed with guilt and unbelief. He's been there. And he's been there before us and without sin for us. He is representatively obeying in faith in our place, in our weakness, in our suffering, and with all of hell's forces arrayed against him.

Today, if you're a Christian you live in the light of God's gracious benediction:

> The LORD bless you and keep you;
> the LORD make his face to shine upon you
>     and be gracious to you;
> the LORD lift up his countenance upon you
>     and give you peace. (Num. 6:24–26)

Those are God's words over us because they were not the words Jesus heard proclaimed over him. The Lord did not bless or keep him. His face did not shine upon him; in fact, the Lord's face was turned away from him. Jesus didn't experience the grace we know every day, even when we're in a time of suffering. And the Father didn't lift up his smile upon him or give him peace. All of this was sacrificed on the mount for you. All of it. For you.

"I thirst" he whispers (John 19:28). We can't imagine the fire of hell that was burning upon his righteous soul or the dryness that overwhelmed his parched throat as he hung there on that tree. Notice this: to the very end he was a human. The man hanging on the cross was not some superhero. He didn't use any special powers to shield himself from what we would experience if we were in his place. Thirsty, hungry, in pain, exhausted, and suffocating as he is unable to expel his breath. He is human to the end.

And finally—after all these years, all these trials, all these hours here in our Egypt of sin and misery—he was able to say with assurance, "It is finished" (John 19:30). He knew that everything that needed to be done for our salvation had been done. He had found us and made us his own. But the food he had come to rely on—"My food is to do the will of him who sent me and to accomplish his work" (4:34)—didn't sustain him in that moment. He had finished the work he had been sent to do, but there was no sign from heaven; even at his birth there had been a star and angels singing.

Yes, the feeding trough had been a meager bed for this King, but should his throne be a bloody cross? Should the sky be silent now? Where were the cries of "Glory to God in the highest" now? Where was the praise for his faithful obedience? Where were the worshiping wise men? They were nowhere to be found. Had he finished the work he had come to do? Yes, he had, but still he could not celebrate, *because death as a sinful man was what he had come to accomplish.*

There was nothing above him but strangely darkened sky. There was nothing beneath him but bloodied mud. There were no shouts of hosanna now; only the weeping of his mother, his female friends, and John mixed in with the groans of the condemned men on either side of him and the taunts of the religious leaders. Yet here he is, continuing to walk by faith and not by sight, praying, "Father, into your hands I commit my spirit!" (Luke 23:46). He entrusted his soul to his Father. His last words were a whispered prayer to his Abba as he "uttered a loud cry and breathed his last" (Mark 15:37). But just to be sure he was really dead, "one of the soldiers pierced his side with a spear, and at once there came out blood and water" (John 19:34). Look upon the one our sins have pierced; behold the man.

Yes, there were miracles at his death. There was an earthquake that tore the curtain in the temple from top to bottom (perhaps caused by the collective shout of the angels), the releasing of souls from the grave, and the probable salvation of a Gentile soul: "And when the centurion, who stood facing him, saw that in this way he breathed his last, he said, 'Truly this man was the Son of God!'" (Mark 15:39). But Jesus didn't get to see any of it. He eyes had already closed in death. Even to the very last moment, he didn't get any special treatment, nothing that would set him apart from you or me. He remained our representative even as he gasped his last breath. *And when his brain died, his memory of all our sin against him died too.*

## THE BURIAL

In his death as in his birth, he remained poor. He didn't own the place where his body would lay. This magnificent human being never did have a place to call his own. Upon his birth he was placed in a borrowed stone feeding trough. Upon his death he was laid in a borrowed stone tomb. In his birth Joseph wrapped him in swaddling cloths. In his death Joseph of Arimathea took his body down from the cross and wrapped him in a linen shroud and "laid him in a tomb that had been cut out of the rock." (Mark 15:46). The rock of ages who was cleft for us, the rock who was "cut out by no human hand," who struck and destroyed all the kingdoms of the earth (Dan. 2:34), was laid tenderly in a tomb to await his decomposition. A cold hard bed for such a gentle man to lie down upon; where were his pillow, his clothing, his cover? And still the heavens were silent.

Was this some cosmic mistake? Had Jesus made an error in judgment? Had things spun out of control, producing an outcome unexpected by all? No, of course not. Here is the testimony of the early church about these events:

> Sovereign Lord, who made the heaven and the earth and the sea and everything in them, who through the mouth of our father David, your servant, said by the Holy Spirit,
>
> > "Why did the Gentiles rage,
> >     and the peoples plot in vain?
> > The kings of the earth set themselves,
> >     and the rulers were gathered together,
> >     against the Lord and against his Anointed"—
>
> for truly in this city there were gathered together against your holy servant Jesus, whom you anointed, both Herod and Pontius Pilate, along with the Gentiles and the peoples of Israel, *to do whatever your hand and your plan had predestined to take place.* (Acts 4:24–28)

Every event of his life from virgin birth to excruciating death were all part of God's plan to bring us to himself. There were no mistakes here. The Romans, the Jews, and Jesus himself did exactly and freely what they were predestined to do: cleanse away sin, bear away wrath, and graft us into him so that we would be forever assured that our exile is over, that we have been found in him.

He was born as a man because he had to be made under the law that we had broken. He had to fulfill all righteousness and suffer and die. He had to be made able to sympathize with all the infirmities of his people and be united to us in a common nature. Thus, the one who purifies us from sin, both as guilt and as pollution, and we who are purified are and must be of the same nature. "Since therefore the children share in flesh and blood, he himself likewise partook of the same" (Heb. 2:14).

At the very darkest moment of his life, when he was suffering more than anyone had ever suffered or would ever suffer again, when he should have been vindicated by his Father and rescued by angels, the heavens were brass, and yet he obeyed! Oh, glorious obedience! In all the days when I'm filled with despair because of my sin, and when I can't find God if my life depended on it; when I give up in fear, doubt, guilt, and despair, I have his righteousness— a righteousness that was lived out for me, on my behalf, and upon which I can rest. Oh, thank you, glorious God. Having loved us, he loved us to the end.

## FOUND IN HIM

Rather than give you a series of questions to consider, let me encourage you to take time in prayer and reflection to ask the Holy Spirit to comfort and assure your heart in whatever way he would.

1) Consider the words to this old hymn, as you think of his great love for you:

> Jesus, Refuge of the weary,
> Object of the spirit's love,
> Fountain in life's desert dreary,
> Savior from the world above.
> O how oft Thine eyes, offended,

Gaze upon the sinner's fall;
Yet upon the cross extended,
Thou didst bear the pain of all.

Do we pass that cross unheeding,
Breathing no repentant vow,
Though we see Thee wounded, bleeding,
See Thy thorn encircled brow?
Yet Thy sinless death hath brought us
Life eternal, peace, and rest;
Only what Thy grace hath taught us
Calms the sinner's stormy breast.

Jesus, may our hearts be burning
With more fervent love for Thee;
May our eyes be ever turning
To Thy cross of agony;
Till in glory, parted never
From the blessèd Savior's side,
Graven in our hearts forever,
Dwell the cross, the Crucified.[1]

2) Summarize what you have learned in this chapter.

# 6

# Jesus Shall Reign

*If Christ has not been raised, your faith is futile.*

1 CORINTHIANS 15:17

Cold, dark, lifeless rock was the bier upon which his body lay. This is the very body the eternal Word took to himself in the womb of his virgin mother, Mary. This is the body that grew from infancy through childhood and adolescence to adulthood. These are the hands that touched the dead, broke bread, and healed the blind. Here are the feet, now deformed by profound injury, swollen, bloodied feet that once traversed miles to quench the thirst of a Samaritan sinner, feet that still retained a faint aroma of pure nard—anointing oil was never so needful before. Here is the mouth, closed, cold—a mouth once so warm with smiles, with laughter, and uncommon truth. Dear face, mutilated, blood-caked—where had his beard gone? Dear eyes—eyes that could look into your heart—now closed. Touch his body. Feel it: inert, stiff, lifeless, pale, cold. This is the work our hands have wrought.

Why this silence? Where is the heartbeat that had begun so many years ago in Mary's womb? How is it that his heart of flesh now resembles a heart of stone? Why this? Must he follow us here too? Yes, he must suffer this as well because he is our husband, our representative. He must undergo the humiliation of death because he must be tempted "in every respect" as we are, yet without sin (Heb. 4:15). He must live and die as dust so that he will fully know what it is for us to be mere dust (Ps. 103:14). Here we see Jesus, who will one day be crowned with glory and honor "because of the suffering of death, so that by the grace of God he might taste death for everyone" (Heb. 2:9). This is the grace of God—he tasted death for you and me. Think of it: "There in the dark vault, lies the body of the Lord of Heaven, soulless! O what depth of humiliation!"[1]

## WHISTLING IN THE DARK

Hours pass by. The hearts of the religious leaders are deeply troubled. "What if his disciples come and steal his body away? What if our fears come about and the disciples tell lies about him?" So they made requests of Pilate and were satisfied by his response—again.

> "You have a guard of soldiers. Go, make it as secure as you can."
> So they went and made the tomb secure by sealing the stone and
> setting a guard. (Matt. 27:65–66)

What had they to fear from this lifeless lump of clay? And why would the power brokers fear these disciples—that spineless gang of no repute? Had they discovered them to be cunning, devious, or influential? Hardly. Didn't they know that they were hiding out in fear even while the Pharisees schemed? No, the Pharisees' guilty hearts started at the sound of every little noise because they knew they had murdered an innocent man (see Prov. 28:1). Their guilty consciences drove them to send security out around the tomb, as if a few soldiers and a rock could keep God in the grave. Even in his death, they felt his presence. Jesus was wielding the axe that was already laid to the root of their tree (Matt. 3:10), and try to ward off his blows as they might, their whole house was about to be left to them desolate (23:38).

## AN ERRAND OF MERCY

Finally the Sabbath had passed; the day of rest was over. Some of the women who loved him had seen the tomb where his body had been placed, and so very early on Sunday, the first day of the week, they got about their gruesome errand and went to do what they could for what was left of him. They would go and anoint his decomposing body so that it would be spared the greatest humiliation of all: the putrefying stench of rotting flesh. They could not stop his suffering; they had been powerless against the humiliation of his execution, but they were determined to do what they could to preserve at least one last shred of his dignity. They would seek to hide the final insult: the foul dissolution of his flesh. Dust we are, to dust we all return—or so they thought.

"Who will roll away the stone for us from the entrance to the tomb?" they wondered as they went on their way with spices and ointments (Mark 16:3). Good question. Surely these women were too weak to move it, and they knew the temple guards wouldn't be of any help. Like us, their poor hearts were troubled with anxieties over practicalities: *How can we roll away the stone? How can we stop his body from smelling while it decays?* Had they never heard him say, "After three days . . ." (Matt. 12:40; Mark 8:31; 9:31; 10:34; John 2:19)? Of course they had, but they hadn't understood it anymore than we would.

## DEATH AND LIFE IN ANOTHER GARDEN

Imagine this setting: it's a chilly morning in a garden graveyard outside of Jerusalem. Roman military guards who had been assigned to watch over the tomb were undoubtedly trying to keep warm while they hoped for reassignment. Suddenly, there was a great earthquake, and an "angel of the Lord descended from heaven and came and rolled back the stone and sat on it" (Matt. 28:2). For a moment the veil between earth and heaven opened, and the earth shook. The angel flicked aside the stone the women had been so worried about and sat on it. "His appearance was like lightning, and his clothing white as snow" (v. 3). Apparently, light is the garb of heaven.[2] Soldiers passed out from fright; women trembled. In his death as in his birth, the pride of the mighty is humbled, and the humble are exalted (Luke 1:51–53).

INCARNATION

Ignoring the sleeping soldiers, the angel said to the women, "Do not be afraid, for I know that you seek Jesus who was crucified. He is not here, for he has risen, as he said. Come see the place where he lay" (Matt. 28:5–6). Encouraged by the angel's beckoning hand, the women bent down to peer into the tomb, and although he had told them that he would certainly arise from the dead, and although they loved him and believed that he only spoke the truth, they fully expected to see only his enshrouded remains. There simply were no categories to describe the shock they felt at what they saw: the tomb—*it was empty!* Gone was the body they had come to anoint. Noticeable by its absence was the stench they fully expected to smell. Nothing of his presence had been left except his neatly folded grave clothes. The tomb is empty? The tomb is empty!

Through their shock the women hear the angels announcing good news again. "Why do you seek the living among the dead?" the angels asked (Luke 24:5). The living among the dead? But we saw him die! *Yes, of course you did, but don't you know? Didn't you believe what he said? How could it be that the Son who is life itself should be held in the grip of death? Do you still not understand that this man you've come to anoint is the God we've worshiped through the ages? How could you not see that it is impossible for this life to cease, for if it did, the creation that is upheld by his power would cease too?* So the women, "went out and fled from the tomb, for trembling and astonishment had seized them, and they said nothing to anyone, for they were afraid" (Mark 16:8).

Shocked and amazed, the women ran from the tomb with "fear and great joy." While they were on their way to tell their brothers what they had seen, they came upon an unexpected traveler. "Greetings!" he said. It was Jesus! Their response? "They came up and took hold of his feet and worshiped him." Of course they did. Here was their friend, their Messiah, their Savior, their King! He wasn't dead! He didn't need their help to preserve his dignity. When they saw him, they fell at his feet and worshiped. There they were hanging onto him—in joyful worship, in fear that he might disappear from their sight. Listen to what Jesus said to them: "Do not be afraid; go and tell my brothers to go to Galilee, and there they will see me" (Matt. 28:8–10). *Do not be afraid. You can go and tell others what you've seen. You all will see me again.* Kind Lord. Loving brother. Gentle husband. Spread the news.

So they went and told the disciples what they had seen: Jesus had risen! To most of the disciples this sounded like nothing more than an "idle tale" (Luke 24:11) told by overwrought women. But when Peter and John heard this message—*Could it be?*—they leapt up and ran to the tomb. John arrived at the tomb first, and looking in he "saw and believed" (John 20:8). Peter arrived on his heels and ran right into the tomb itself. It was true! He was gone! What were they to do now? They still didn't know. Yes, Jesus had been raised, but they hadn't been commissioned yet, so in fear of the retribution of the Pharisees, they returned home, wondering how what they saw would eventually intersect with their lives.

## HEALING THE BROKENHEARTED

One woman arrived after the others had left. Her heart had been broken. She wouldn't accompany the other women as they had gone to anoint his body. She couldn't face it, so she went along at her own pace, weeping the bitterest tears she had ever known. *How could he have died? What is left now? How can I even take a breath? Oh, Lord, how could you die? Why didn't you save yourself?* Finally she arrived at the garden where he was entombed, and an even greater grief overwhelmed her. *Wasn't it bad enough that he had been murdered? Did they have to desecrate his body by stealing it too?*

> But Mary stood weeping outside the tomb, and as she wept she stooped to look into the tomb. And she saw two angels in white, sitting where the body of Jesus had lain. . . . They said to her, "Woman, why are you weeping?" She said to them, "They have taken away my Lord, and I do not know where they have laid him." Having said this, she turned around and saw Jesus standing,

117

but she did not know that it was Jesus. Jesus said to her, "Woman, why are you weeping? Whom are you seeking?" Supposing him to be the gardener, she said to him, "Sir, if you have carried him away, tell me where you have laid him, and I will take him away." Jesus said to her, "Mary." (John 20:11–16)

"Mary." How many times had she heard that dear mouth form her name? "Mary." She had loved it when he had first spoken it to her, when he had first welcomed her—a troubled woman who had never been welcomed like that by a man before. "Mary." And as their relationship grew, she grew more and more fond of the way he said it. The sound of that voice had been permanently preserved in her memory. But her grief had taught her that she would never hear it again, so how is it that the sound of it had entered her ears once more? "Mary." That's all he needed to say, and she was completely sure. No one said "Mary" like he did, and she knew immediately. *He's not dead! He's here again! Oh, now I will hang on to him so tightly that I will never lose him again!*

Mary's response, like her sisters before her, was to cling to him. That's how you would have responded, too. She thought he had been taken from her, and now she is determined she will never let him go. *Oh, brokenhearted sister. He will never leave you again! Soon you'll be convinced of his resurrection and you'll know the truth of his promised presence by his Spirit.* But she must let his body go, for he must ascend to his Father. He surely welcomed her touch, but he would not allow himself to be kept in her grip alone. He was hers, but he also belonged to heaven and to all of us.

"Go to my brothers and say to them, 'I am ascending to my Father and your Father, to my God and your God'" (John 20:17). Can you hear his patient heart? His exquisite inclusiveness? These men who deserted him are his brothers! His Father is their Father! His God is their God! What joy! What astonishing grace!

Consider again the great condescension and love of our Savior. No impatience do we see here; no, "Where were they while I suffered?" Nor even a "What did you *think* I meant when I told you

I would die and be raised on the third day?" No, never a word of rebuke or condemnation. This is the risen King, and what does he have to say? Tell them that I am their brother and that we have the same Father! In his heart is just kind condescension and patient love. "My God and Father is now your God and Father because I am now and forever will be your brother."

## HE COULD NOT BE BOUND BY DEATH

He had been bound by death, as death binds us all, but death would not be victorious over him. Death's ultimate degradation, the decomposition of the body, was not part of Jesus's necessary obedience. The Father would not allow his beloved Son to undergo decay. In fact, it was impossible that the body he had taken to himself should dissolve—for it was this very body that he would animate once again into life eternal as he led his bride forth from her grave into new life.

> And so—and at last—in response to His Son's "It is finished!" the Father thundered an
> "Amen!" from heaven, and Jesus's heart began to beat once more.

In that one instant the inevitability of the death and deconstruction that had been the trajectory of all humanity since our dreadful fall screeched to a halt. A great reversal had begun. A great harvest day had commenced since that "grain of wheat" had fallen into the ground and died (John 12:24). A new race of men and women were born, a new race of beloved ones recreated in the image of God. A new humanity who will never die had come to life.

> God raised him up, loosing the pangs of death, because it was not possible for him to be held by it. . . . "For you will not abandon my soul to Hades, or let your Holy One see corruption. . . ." [David] foresaw and spoke about the resurrection of the Christ, that he was not abandoned to Hades, nor did his flesh see corruption. This Jesus God raised up. (Acts 2:24, 27, 31–32)

Peter preached that God had loosed his Son from the "pangs of death." These death pangs speak of the pain and labor of birth. Although it might seem strange to us, we can say that in his death and resurrection Jesus is giving birth; he felt the pangs of death, he labored to bring forth offspring. In fact, he said something like this in John 16 when he was talking to his disciples about his impending death and the sorrow that they would feel—sorrow that would be turned to joy, just as a woman has sorrow as she labors and her pains are upon her:

> But when she has delivered the baby, she no longer remembers the anguish, for joy that a human being has been born into the world. (John 16:21)

Out of his tomb that was a womb, a new creation comes forth. He has been born anew, but this time he is not alone. He is both the one being born and the one giving birth, for in his new life he brings with him all the children God had given him (Heb. 2:13). As Jesus himself was born into deathless life, he was also the first-fruits of a new humanity. In his birth from death, he brought with him all of his brothers of whom he was "not ashamed" (Heb. 2:11).

> Of his own will he *brought us forth* by the word of truth, that we should be a kind of firstfruits of his creatures. (James 1:18; see also 1 Cor. 15:20, 23)

Again, it may seem odd to think in these terms, but in the resurrection and empty tomb a true birth has occurred, and just as when the head of a baby appears, and you know that soon you will see the rest of the body, so our Head has appeared, who speaks greetings to us so that we can know without doubt that we too will follow him out of the grave. "Greetings!" What is your name? He speaks it now: "Mary" or "Elyse" or "_____"! Supply your name and know that the risen Lord is greeting you!

We're not the only ones rejoicing now either, for it is with great joy that "he shall see his offspring," just as Isaiah prophesied

(Isa. 53:10). We are that offspring. He has brought us forth—given birth—to us! And just as a woman forgets her pain for the "joy that a human being has been born into the world" (John 16:21), so it is that with great joy he will sing his Father's praise "in the midst of the [heavenly] congregation" (Heb. 2:12). What will he sing?

> Sing, O barren one, who did not bear;
>> break forth into singing and cry aloud,
>> you who have not been in labor!
> For the children of the desolate one will be more
>> than the children of her who is married. (Isa. 54:1)

When we read that God's ways are higher than our ways (Isa. 55:9), we really don't have much of a clue what that means, do we? Think of it: a virgin shall conceive. A desolate unmarried man sings because he gives birth and sees his children. A new humanity is born in a new garden, but this time it is not from the dust of the earth but from the flesh of God, once dead but now alive, that they come. God labors! The Son cries out in pain, and we are born again! He thought nothing of the shame of the cross because of the joy of our birth in him (Heb. 12:2).

## OF FIRST IMPORTANCE

Now I would remind you, brothers, of the gospel I preached to you, which you received, in which you stand, and by which you are being saved, if you hold fast to the word I preached to you— unless you believed in vain.

For I delivered to you as of first importance what I also received: that Christ died for our sins in accordance with the Scriptures, that he was buried, that he was raised on the third day in accordance with the Scriptures, and that he appeared to Cephas, then to the twelve. Then he appeared to more than five hundred brothers at one time, most of whom are still alive, though some have fallen asleep. Then he appeared to James, then to all the apostles. Last of all, as to one untimely born, he appeared also to me. . . . If Christ has not been raised, your faith is futile. (1 Cor. 15:1–8, 17)

This is the glorious good news. This is the good news in which you must continually stand. This is the message that must be constantly preached: the God-man, Jesus Christ, died for our sins, was buried, and was raised on the third day![3] There is no other message that we need to hear, no other message that will enable us to stand.

And stand we will, because we have assurances that this message is true. We know that it is true because there are witnesses to these events. Aside from the women who gave testimony to the empty tomb, the apostle Paul writes that there were numbers of people who saw the Lord after he had risen: Cephas, the twelve, five hundred brothers, James, all the apostles, and finally Paul himself. Let's take a moment now to think of these events and to draw out of them assurances that our faith is not in vain.

## WITNESSES ON THE ROAD

Before Jesus appeared to Peter, he met two disciples walking on the road to Emmaus. You remember that we discussed this event in chapter 1 and how, during this appearance, Jesus taught his hopeless disciples how to interpret the Bible (Luke 24:13–27). It was during this discussion that Jesus called them "slow of heart to believe" and asked them, "Was it not necessary that the Christ should suffer these things and enter into his glory?" (vv. 25–26). But it was not until they ate together, when "he took the bread and blessed and broke it and gave it to them," that "their eyes were opened, and they recognized him" (vv. 30–31). What had they seen when he broke bread for them? Perhaps it was only then that they saw his nail-scarred hands, and then they knew. This was Jesus! The infallible interpreter had just given them a lesson in hermeneutics, but it was when they saw his wounded hands and fed them with bread that they were convinced and said, "The Lord has risen!" (v. 34).

## A HUMBLED WITNESS

The last time we saw Peter (Cephas), he had what some people might call a really good confession. He had been proclaiming his fidelity and willingness to stand for his friend, the one he had rightly identified as the Messiah. If anyone's faith-filled confession should have brought about a great success story, it should have been Peter's. Later, though, we find a mute Peter warming himself by a fire while his brother was being accused of blasphemy. Where was Peter's great confession now? It had turned to dust in his mouth. He denied that he even knew the man. And then, afterward, when he had finally seen himself in the mirror of Jesus's words, he had gone out to weep bitterly—a failure who had just wasted three years of his life believing in a man who turned out to be a condemned criminal. All his delusions of grandeur had gone up in the smoke rising from that courtyard fire.

Then Jesus looked at him as he was being led away, and for the first time in his life, Peter finally knew himself. It was in God's light that he saw the light of who he really was (Ps. 36:9), and what he saw crushed him and drove him to despair. He hadn't been strong enough even to stand with his friend during his final hours. Peter had been completely stripped of all that he had trusted in. He didn't need a good confession; he needed a realistic theology. He needed to shed his theology of glory and replace it with a theology of death and resurrection.[4]

## TIME FOR RECONCILIATION

John recorded what happened when Jesus revealed himself again to the disciples by the Sea of Tiberius (John 21:1–19). Before the disciples' commissioning at Pentecost, Peter and the others had been marking time; they didn't know what they were supposed to be doing, and they didn't have the power to do anything more than hide out and question one another about what the resurrection might mean.

Ever the man of action, Peter got bored as he sat with some of the disciples. *I'm not going to just sit around here and do nothing*, he thought. So he said to his friends, "I am going fishing" (John 21:3). And since none of them had anything else to do, they agreed that they would go with him. Maybe after all the three years they had spent with Jesus was going to turn out as nothing more than an interesting intermission from their life as fishermen. Maybe they could start up their fishing businesses again. But this too would turn out to be another vain endeavor, for after fishing all night they had caught nothing. Now they were not only bored but also cold and hungry.

Then, just as day was breaking, Jesus stood on the shore. He called out to them, "Children, do you have any fish?" and they replied, "No" (John 21:5). So he instructed them to cast their nets on the other side of the boat, and instantly the nets were so full that they weren't able to pull them in. John recognized that the man on the shore was the Lord and told Peter. Never one to wait around to consider the wisest course of action, Peter grabbed his cloak and threw himself into the water. *I'll show him how much I love him! I'll show him that I'm truly sorry and willing to prove my love for him!*

Of course, it's Jesus who is busy proving his love for his disciples now. When they all had finally arrived at the shore, they saw that Jesus had laid out a charcoal fire, and he invited them to cook some of the fish for breakfast. The risen Lord cared that these men have warm food after such a disappointing night of labor. He fed them breakfast. Think of that.

Then, perhaps putting his arm around his errant friend, Jesus took Peter aside for a short walk and asked him, "Simon, son of John, do you love me more than these?" (John 21:15). *Do you love me more than these men do? Do you love me more than you love your reputation among them? How's that good confession working out for you now, Peter? Do you still think your love for me is unassailable?*

In fact, Jesus queried Simon three times about his love, and after answering in the affirmative twice Peter finally admitted, "Lord, you know everything; you know that I love you" (John 21:17). Yes, Peter did love Jesus, but he also knew that Jesus was able to determine the quality of his love far better than Peter was. Before Peter had argued with the Lord about his ability to evaluate his heart. Now he argued no longer. No longer was Peter so full of himself. No longer did he think he knew his own strength better than the Lord knew it. Peter did know that he loved Jesus, but he also believed (finally!) that Jesus knew what was in his heart. Jesus and Peter were reconciled. How loving and kind of the Lord to seek out his errant friend and restore him to a place of relationship and ministry.

Peter's testimony about the resurrection would eventually cost him his life. This man who had been terrified of a little servant girl would ultimately die a martyr's death, so convinced was he by what he had seen: his friend, the Christ, yet lived and had sought him out for reconciliation! So it was on the day of Pentecost that Peter preached, "This Jesus God raised up, and of that we all are witnesses" (Acts 2:32). Later in Jerusalem he proclaimed, "And you killed the Author of life, whom God raised from the dead. To this we are witnesses" (3:15). And to the Gentile Cornelius's household he said,

> And we are witnesses of all that he [Jesus] did both in the country of the Jews and in Jerusalem. They put him to death by hanging him on a tree, but God raised him on the third day and made him to appear. (Acts 10:39–40)

Peter's life was transformed by the reality of the resurrection. He became a witness.

## DO NOT DOUBT

On different occasions Jesus appeared to other disciples. He continually told them not to be afraid and proved to them that he wasn't a spirit by showing them his nail-scarred hands and feet. "Touch me, and see," he told them. "Have you anything here to eat?" he asked them and they gave him a piece of broiled fish, and he took it and ate before them (Luke 24:36–43). Loving Lord. Ever the servant, he did all these things so that they—and through their testimony, we—would believe.

He even condescended to answer the doubts of his friend Thomas. *I won't believe unless I see the marks on his body*, he had vowed. So, what does the Savior do? He said to Thomas, "Put your finger here, and see my hands; and put out your hand, and place it in my side. Do not disbelieve, but believe" (John 20:27). Jesus doesn't despise doubters. No, he speaks peace to them and grants them eyes to see and faith to believe.

> Thomas answered him, "My Lord and my God!" Jesus said to him, "Have you believed because you have seen me? Blessed are those who have not seen and yet have believed." (John 20:28–29)

## ONE UNTIMELY BORN

The last apostle to see the risen Christ was one who hated him. Jesus appeared to Saul when Saul was on his way to have Christians arrested and thrown in prison. Why? Because they were preaching the resurrection!

> Now as he went on his way, he approached Damascus, and suddenly a light from heaven shone around him. And falling to the ground he heard a voice saying to him, "Saul, Saul, why are you persecuting me?" And he said, "Who are you, Lord?" And he said, "I am Jesus, whom you are persecuting." (Acts 9:3–5)

As was the case with the rest of the apostles, Paul's theology was significantly impacted by his encounter with the risen Christ. It was, in fact, the most important encounter he had ever had, and he would later say that without the resurrection, his faith in Jesus Christ—his entire life—would prove to be in vain (1 Cor. 15:14).

## LET US CONSIDER AND KEEP CONSIDERING THE RESURRECTION

With Paul, we cannot overestimate the significance of the resurrection for our lives. In the chapters to come, you'll see more clearly how the resurrection of the God-man impacts our lives, but for now, here are some important points.

First, the resurrection proves the validity of Christ's claims about himself. When someone is able to come back from the dead, after telling you that was what he was going to do, it's a good idea to believe other things he has to say about himself. For instance, he said that he and the Father are one, that before Abraham existed he was, that he is the light, the bread, the living water, the good shepherd, and the vine. He said that he is sinless and that everything he did was done for only one reason: to please his Father. He said that he had come from his Father and would return to his Father, bringing with him everyone his Father had given him. If anyone else said these sorts of things, they would be committed to an asylum. But we can trust that Jesus's claims are true because he rose from the dead.

The resurrection assures us that Jesus's unique teaching was also true. Rather than dumbing down the law's demands, making them manageable, he heightened them, making them completely unattainable. Every truth he taught was antithetical to what the religious leaders of his day (and ours!) taught: you can't work your way to heaven; you'll never be good enough. You simply need to give up and believe. "What must we do, to be doing the works of God?" he was asked. His answer: "This is the work of God, that you believe in him whom he has sent" (John 6:28–29). On the morning of the resurrection, even the angels themselves attested to the veracity of his claims: "He is not here, for he is risen, *as he said*" (Matt. 28:6).

## THE CURSE OF DEATH IS BROKEN

Simply put, the only way we can know that believing in Jesus will bring eternal life and forgiveness of sins is that God raised him from the dead, proving that the curse of death for disobedience, which had been humanity's inheritance since the fall, had been annihilated. God accepted Jesus's obedience on our behalf and then raised him from the dead to prove that the curse that had hung over us had been replaced by blessing. We have been forgiven, and eternal life has been granted to us, for "if Christ has not been raised, your faith is futile and you are still in your sins" (1 Cor. 15:17). The fact of the resurrection proves that our faith is not mere wishful thinking; there are enough proofs of the resurrection to overcome all our doubts—not the least of which is the reality that every one of the prominent people who were witnesses of the resurrection were so impacted by it that it changed the direction of their life, and many of them were willing to suffer martyrdom because of it.

We can be confident that we will be with Jesus because, as he was the Son who was the firstborn from the grave, he has promised to take us with him, so that wherever he is, we may be also. He was exiled to death to bring us from our exile in death to life and relationship with him.

## OUR ASCENDED BROTHER-KING

He presented himself alive to them after his suffering by many proofs, appearing to them during forty days and speaking about the kingdom of God. . . . As they were looking on, he was lifted up, and a cloud took him out of their sight. (Acts 1:3, 9)

Forty days after his resurrection, the God-man, Jesus the Christ, returned to his Father's throne. The joy in the Son's heart at this reunion cannot be overstated. He was going home. He had done it all! He would see his Father's glory again. The earthly ministry that had begun over thirty years before, that of his traverse through this world of weakness, frailty, and suffering, ended when he ascended. His role as the deliverer who brought his people out of this Egypt, became their Passover Lamb, and led them to dry ground through the Red Sea of his blood was finally complete. He had done it. It was finished!

It's important to note that his ascension occurred on the Mount of Olives—the place where he had warred with his righteous soul in prayer; here on the Mount of Olives he was completely vindicated, for he had fulfilled his Father's demand of obedience and submission. There, in that garden and still in bodily form, he was taken up from the disciples, and they watched as "a cloud took him out of their sight" (Acts 1:9). We've seen that cloud before, haven't we? This time, though, the cloud came to take the well-pleasing beloved Son home.

It seems to me that the ascension of our Savior is one of the most overlooked parts of his incarnational ministry yet one of the most important. Jesus himself predicted that he would return to where he had come from, to his Father, and his welcome into the holy presence was proof that he had accomplished all the work the Father had given him to do.

From beginning to end, Jesus had been on a covenantal mission to do the work the Father had given him. In the garden of Eden, the Lord had given Adam work to do. He was to keep the garden, guarding it and obeying the Father's demand for obedience, so that he and his offspring might enjoy the tree of life forever. But Adam failed, and death and exile was the inheritance he left for us all. So the Son, the new Adam, had to come. He had to condescend and take upon himself our identity—cursed sinner—so that we might take upon ourselves his identity—obedient Son—and eat once again of the tree of life. When he returned home, it was as the obedient Son who had borne the punishment of the prodigal—for us—for our salvation. And he brings us home with him.

As our ascended King,

> God has highly exalted him and bestowed on him the name that is above every name. (Phil. 2:9)

And:

> He is the head of the body, the church. He is the beginning, the firstborn from the dead, that in everything he might be preeminent. (Col. 1:18)

Yet, exalted King as he is, he is still wearing our flesh! Jesus Christ, the God-man, rules now from heaven as the man, Christ Jesus. Again, think of that! He has so become one with us that he has taken our flesh into the throne room of God, where it had never been before, and he has exalted our humble estate by bringing us along with him into the very presence of God. "Now dust sits at the right hand of the Father!"[5]

Because he is there in heaven as our loving brother and husband, we can be assured of this: we have been "raised" up with Christ and "seated" with him in the heavenly places (Eph. 2:6). We are with him now. He who once was Spirit has now *and forever* become man, and man is now *and forever* welcome into heaven, his home. When we get there, we'll be welcomed because he has already been there preparing a place for us (John 14:2–3). We're no longer lost or wandering. We're home.

But that's not all. Even now he continues to pray for us and prepare a meal for us. In part we do experience this meal and home here, in our churches, but a day is coming when, if we believe, he will reach out a warm, nail-scarred hand of flesh and welcome us home.

> It was *in our nature* that he offered himself to the Father on the cross, and *in our nature* that he ascended far above all things created, and *in our nature* that he lives and reigns forever—in indissoluble personal union. . . . He offered as a sacrifice the flesh he received from us, that he might wipe out our guilt by his act of expiation and appease the Father's righteous wrath.[6]

He has been and will be forever found with us so that we may forever be found with him!

## FOUND IN HIM

1) The angels ask, "Why do you seek the living among the dead?" (Luke 24:5). How often do you do that? How many times have you searched for life among lifeless things? How would remembering the resurrection help you differentiate between the two?

2) Consider the words to this great hymn:

> Jesus shall reign where'er the sun
> Does its successive journeys run;
> His kingdom stretch from shore to shore,
> Till moons shall wax and wane no more.
>
> To Him shall endless prayer be made,
> And endless praises crown His head;
> His name like sweet perfume shall rise
> With every morning sacrifice.
>
> People and realms of every tongue
> Dwell on His love with sweetest song;
> And infant voices shall proclaim
> Their early blessings on His name.
>
> Blessings abound where'er He reigns;
> All prisoners leap and loose their chains;
> The weary find eternal rest,
> And all who suffer want are blest.
>
> Let every creature rise and bring
> honors peculiar to our King;
> angels descend with songs again,
> and earth repeat the loud amen![7]

3) How often do you think about the implications of the resurrection? In particular, how does Jesus's ongoing life intersect with your life in the nitty-gritty of your day?

4) How often do you think about the implications of the ascension? In particular, how does Jesus's ongoing reign as the God-man, who still bears scars and yet rules from heaven, intersect with your life?

5) Summarize in four or five sentences what you learned in this chapter.

PART 2

# UNION WITH CHRIST

# Introduction to Part 2

Up until this time, we've been examining the incarnation, the Word's union with humanity. We've considered how Jesus's earthly life was lived for our benefit and for the glory of his Father. We've delved deeply into his manhood, observing his perfect fulfilling of the law, his substitutionary death on the cross, and his bodily resurrection—a resurrection that, along with his ascension, assures us of our salvation.

From this point on we're going to be spending our time considering the benefits of the work he did, particularly as our representative, brother, and husband. Of course, his primary goal in becoming man and living as he did was to complete the work the Father had given him, but this work also had another goal: to bless us, granting that all the benefits he had earned are now poured out on our unworthy yet beloved souls.

Our gaze will shift now to our union with Christ (and all its benefits), but this is no inconsequential postscript, as John Murray writes:

> Nothing is more central or basic than union and communion with Christ. . . . Union with Christ is really the central truth of the whole doctrine of salvation not only in its application but also in its once-for-all accomplishment in the finished work of Christ.[1]

In shifting your focus from what he has done through the incarnation to how his work impacts us and, in particular, how our oneness with him in all that he has accomplished transforms our identity and life, you need to understand that everything that can (and should) be said about our union with him will not be said. Volumes have been written about our union with Christ, and it is not my intention to try to duplicate others' work. This is not a systematic presentation on union and every implication of union in a believer's life. Rather, my goal is to draw you into a closer and more fully assured recognition of his presence and power in your life and how being "in" him changes everything about you and how you live your life.

7

# "I in Them"

*Blessed be the God and Father of our Lord Jesus Christ,*
*who has blessed us in Christ with every spiritual*
*blessing in the heavenly places, even as he chose us*
*in him before the foundation of the world.*

Ephesians 1:3–4

All the truths of the incarnation and our union with Christ have their genesis in the fact that God the Father chose us to be *in* Jesus, to be one with him, in indissoluble union forever. This union, oneness, or "in-ness" is so very essential to understanding our salvation that it simply cannot be overemphasized.

Thirty-three times in Paul's letters alone he speaks of our being "in Christ" (not counting the times he speaks of union "with him" or "with the Lord"). Even though this "in-ness" is such a recurrent theme in Paul, most of us tend to be unfamiliar with it. So let's take some time now, as we continue our discussion of union, to consider six ways Paul speaks about it in the book of Romans. Because we are one with Jesus we have the following.

## REDEMPTION

Although we "all have sinned" and fallen "short of the glory of God," we are "justified by his grace as a gift, through the *redemption that is in Christ Jesus,* whom God put forward as a propitiation by his blood, to be received by faith" (Rom. 3:23–25). *Redemption* means that God purchased us or bought us back from our bondage to sin and slavery to Satan through the payment of a ransom, which his justice demanded. The very life and blood of Jesus was that ransom payment, as he said: "For even the Son of Man came not to be served but to serve, and to *give his life as a ransom for many* (Mark 10:45; 1 Tim. 2:6). He knew that the blood pumping through his veins had one purpose: to be poured out in payment for our sin. In eternity we will sing songs of worship about the redemption and ransom he purchased, "Worthy are you to take the scroll and to open its seals, *for you were slain, and by your blood you ransomed people for God from every tribe and language and people and nation*" (Rev. 5:9).

## DEAD TO SIN AND ALIVE TO GOD

Another facet of our union with Christ is both symbolized and formalized by baptism. In baptism we have been united with Jesus in his death and resurrection (Rom. 6:3–4), for baptism "symbolizes [our] union with, and incorporation into, Christ."[1] Just as Jesus was buried after his death, in the same way we too are buried with him in baptism. Baptism is the signal before heaven and to our own hearts that we believe that our sin has been paid for.

By our faith, then, we have also died to all of sin's accusatory power, resultant allurements, and enslavement. The ink on our old life's record of debt has been completely washed away; a new record is now ours. Because sin, guilt, and the law no longer hold sway over us, we are free to walk before God in loving, filial relationship—no longer wondering about his disposition to us—no longer exiles fearing his wrath. In this way, just as Jesus was raised from death for sin and from the grave, so we too are raised from baptismal water as completely new people in new relationship with our Father.

In light of this, Paul counsels us, "Consider yourselves dead to sin and alive to God *in* Christ Jesus" (Rom. 6:11). This means that when Jesus died on the cross for our sins, in God's eyes we were there with him. We have already received just punishment for our sins. We have died. We have been to the grave. Every sin that we have ever or will ever commit has already been paid for, not because of our good works or resolution to do better but because we were *in* Christ when he died in payment for our sin.

In placing us in Christ like this, in counting us dead and alive again, the Father has completely transformed our relationship with him. We are now no longer dead but are *alive* to him, because death for sin, the curse for disobedience that had hung over us since Eden, has been satisfied. Death's insatiable maw was glutted by Christ's blood.

No longer laboring under a curse for our incessant disobedience, we are now free to obey (yet fail to obey) as blessed, beloved children. We are no longer enslaved to sin's temptations, because all the guilt and resultant hatred of God and his law has been obliterated. Rather than simply telling ourselves that we ought to do better, to resist temptation, it is by remembering our union with Jesus on the cross that we are transformed: set at liberty to love righteousness and the God who has given it to us. Our former relationship with God as the just judge whom we despised (who demanded an obedience we were unable and unwilling to accomplish) has been transformed into that of a loving Father who gladly welcomes us as his Son's flawed yet beautiful bride.

This alteration in relationship with the Father changes everything about how we approach the battle against sin and obedience to the law; bondage to the law's demands as a way to secure relationship *always* elicits a sinful response on our part (Rom. 7:5), but because we have already paid the penalty for disobedience to the law and completely fulfilled all its demands in Christ, sin and the law no longer control us. God loves and welcomes us. We no longer owe payment for our sin. Jesus paid it all.

In addition, just like Jesus, we have been vindicated by the resurrection. God's renewed smile after the fury and punishment of the cross shows that Jesus's offering and life's work had been given the Father's stamp of approval. Again, the resurrection is

66

666666

God's "Amen" to Christ's "It is finished!" But that's not all. The resurrection is also God's "Amen" to our "It is finished, for I believe that when he died, I died, and when he rose, I arose; I believe that you have forgiven me and made me righteous and will raise me up on the last day."

Our entire lives—our sin, our good works, our faith, our doubt, everything, in fact—have been subsumed into him in the resurrection, and we now stand before God alive, not dead, cleansed, not vile, whole, not shattered, and welcomed, not sent away. We stand in complete righteousness and holiness, no longer dead in our trespasses but completely and eternally alive in him. We are invited to live our whole life under his benediction, his smile, his love.[2]

## ETERNAL LIFE

"For the wages of sin is death, but the free gift of God is eternal life in Christ Jesus our Lord" (Rom. 6:23). The end of all the work we have accomplished on our own, all our supposed good deeds, all our secret sins, all our cavalier apathy, all our ignorance, diligence, self-righteousness, self-control, arrogance, friendliness, back stabbing, idolatry, and unbelief—the end of all that we can and have done apart from our union with Christ—is death. The result or fruit of our lives, of those things of which we are now ashamed, is death (v. 21).

What kind of death is this? Certainly there are plenty of arrogant idolaters strolling around in blissful unbelief today. They certainly seem alive, but they're not. The spiritual death that the Bible talks about is not usually immediate or physical at our first act of rebellion but is, rather, the death that has permeated our race since the first Adam's disobedience in the garden of Eden. You'll remember how the Lord promised that on the day Adam sinned, he would die (Gen. 2:17); and even though he didn't die physically on that day, he and every one of his progeny are immersed in a world of death from conception.

What kind of death is this? It is exile, banishment from God's presence and from his goodness. It is the wandering, lostness, futility, and judgment that has affected us all. Yes, of course it is the ultimate dissolution of our physical bodies; we are all dying right now, whether we juice organic vegetables or not; we've all been diagnosed with a terminal illness. But this death is also the dissolution of our personality, marked as it is by an absence of lasting happiness, a continual dissatisfaction with what we have, the insatiable desire for more, a terrifying recognition that we're not what we should be, all followed by full-tilt hypocrisy and masquerade. This death is marked by a constant desire to somehow get back to the "good old days," which is actually an innate desire within us all for Eden and God himself, to have relationship with him, to be welcomed to walk with him again in the cool of the day.

But it is also a spiritual death, an eternal separation from God that will be so horrific that it can only be described in the most terrifying of terms: eternal fire that will never fully consume us but will instead continue to burn forever to our unspeakable torment, while we wail over the awareness that we've made a fatal mistake from which we will never recover. Why such a terrible punishment? Because of the great value of the Son we have spurned.

But because we are in union with Christ, we are no longer reaping the wages that our sin has earned for us. No, instead we've been given God's free gift: eternal life. Notice how death is something we work for—it is our wage—but eternal life is not something we're able to earn. It is too costly; we can't pay that price. It is a gift given to us in Christ. If we have it, it is only because Jesus earned it for us and has given it to us.

Because we are united to him, we are recipients of all the indescribable blessings that belong to Christ. As the God-man, he is welcomed to heaven and seated at the right hand of the Father, who rejoices over him. But here's the amazing news: we are, too! He is completely loved, approved of, accepted, and delighted in, and so are we. Although our physical bodies will die (if Jesus does

141

UNION WITH CHRIST

not return first), we will never taste or see death, for just at the
moment it begins to clutch us, he will come and take our souls to
himself. He can do this because he has conquered death. Eternal
life is the life we have now, a life full of blessing and the unimagi-
nable joy of knowing that we forever will be loved by him.

## FREEDOM FROM CONDEMNATION

In Romans 6 Paul describes the life of faith—a life characterized
by an ongoing recognition that we are dead to sin and alive to
God—and what that life should look like. But in Romans 7 Paul
describes his own life, which is characterized by his struggle with
sin. It is a struggle that is summarized in this way:

> For I do not understand my own actions. For I do not do what I
> want, but I do the very thing that I hate. . . . For I have the desire
> to do what is right, but not the ability to carry it out. For I do not
> do the good I want, but the evil I do not want is what I keep on
> doing. . . . Wretched man that I am! Who will deliver me from
> this body of death? (Rom. 7:15, 18–19, 24)

What is Paul's answer to his anguished quest for deliverance?
Instead of pulling out his hair and slumping down in despair or
making a list of how to have his best life now, he sings, "Thanks
be to God through Jesus Christ our Lord!" (Rom. 7:25). It is Jesus
who will deliver him from his demoralizing failure as he struggles with sin, not his own efforts, not his New Year's resolutions,
not by measuring his forward progress in getting his spiritual act
together. Jesus alone is Paul's deliverer, and it is because Paul is
assured of ultimate deliverance that he can declare (oh, precious
words!), "There is therefore now no condemnation for those who
are in Christ Jesus" (8:1). When? Now. Why? Because God has
already condemned our sin in the human flesh of his own Son.

> For God has done what the law, weakened by the flesh, could not
> do. By sending his own Son in the likeness of sinful flesh and for
> sin, he condemned sin in the flesh, in order that the righteous

142

requirement of the law might be fulfilled in us, who walk not according to the flesh but according to the Spirit. (Rom. 8:3–4)

The threat of condemnation, the judgment of a just God who sees past our righteous pretensions, the wrath that abides on all who disregard his commandments—all of that condemnation is completely, utterly obliterated because we are in Jesus, and he already bore it all. He drank it all down, took it all into himself, and was crushed under it for us so that we would be completely free to love him and be loved by him.

## FREEDOM FROM THE LAW OF SIN AND DEATH

In Jesus we have been set free from the principle of sin and death. This liberation from the principle or law of sin and death has come to us through our union with Jesus who has given us life (1 Cor. 15:45). "For the law of the Spirit of life has set you free *in* Christ Jesus from the law of sin and death" (Rom. 8:2). The continual cycle of sin and death that marked our response to the demands of the law has been broken *because our failures have been recast as Christ's obediences.* We have been given Christ's perfect record of always having obeyed, and, second, we have been given a new heart, a heart like his, one that desires to obey out of love. This is the transformation that God promised us through Ezekiel:

> I will sprinkle clean water on you, and you shall be clean from all your uncleannesses, and from all your idols I will cleanse you. And I will give you a new heart, and a new spirit I will put within you. And I will remove the heart of stone from your flesh and give you a heart of flesh. And I will put my Spirit within you, and cause you to walk in my statutes and be careful to obey my rules. (Ezek. 36:25–27)

The humanly unbreakable pattern of law-sin-death, law-sin-death has been shattered because we are now in union with him. He took that law-sin-death pattern and obliterated it by obeying the law, shunning every sin, dying in our place, and then being raised victorious over it. In him law-obedience-life is the pattern that marks our lives.

## THE LOVE OF GOD

*Our union with Christ may be summed up in these words: because the Father has immeasurable love for the Son, he has immeasurable love for us.* He has immeasurable love for us because we are *in* the Son, part of him, one with him, married to him, part of the family. He looks at us as though we always were. When the Father looks at us, he doesn't scratch his head and wonder, "How did she get in here? What's he doing here?" No, he says, "This is my beloved daughter, my beloved son, in whom I am well pleased." All because we are in union with the Son he loves.

If you've ever doubted God's love for you, it is because you aren't thinking about his love for his Son. Does his love for his Son ever change? Does it wax and wane depending on the Father's moods? No, of course not. *In addition, our "one with-ness" in him is eternal and unbreakable; our union with him is his holy vow that he will be one with us forever. Cease loving you? God can no more do that than he can cease loving his own dear Son. You're loved. You're not alone or lost. You've been found in him.*

## PAUL'S DESCRIPTION OF OUR
## UNION WITH CHRIST

*Yes, because of this "one with-ness," we have redemption, eternal life, no condemnation, freedom from slavery to the principle of sin and death, and the never-ending love of God.* In addition, we also have unity with the Godhead and with other members of the church; we have grace, wisdom, righteousness, sanctification, and redemption. We are his new creation, reconciled with God and led in triumphal procession over our enemies. Because we are in Christ, we are justified and inherit all the blessings of Abraham. We have been given eternal life and are completely free from the condemnation that our disobedience to the law had produced. We've been freed from having to merit God's love through obedience and have been assured of his love for us, no matter how we fail. We are one body with him, dear adopted children, and have every spiritual blessing in him. In fact, right now we've been raised up and seated with him, enabled to do good works that he has already accomplished for us. We have forgiveness of sins, life, grace, and salvation, and every need has been supplied.[3] This union, this "in-ness" that we have with him, is what the Christian life is all about!

## WE ARE HIS TEMPLE, A HOLY BUILDING

Here's another analogy that might be helpful in understanding what our union with Christ is like: Paul calls us God's temple, the place where the Holy Spirit dwells (1 Cor. 3:16). This metaphor of a building that has been joined together is seen particularly in Ephesians 2:19–22, where Paul uses the analogy of a building that is alive, a structure that actually grows:

> So then you are no longer strangers and aliens, but you are fellow citizens with the saints and members of the household of God, built on the foundation of the apostles and prophets, Christ Jesus himself being the cornerstone, in whom the whole structure, being joined together, grows into a holy temple in the Lord. In him you also are being built together into a dwelling place for God by the Spirit.

This building is erected upon Jesus himself, who has "become the cornerstone" (Acts 4:11). Jesus Christ, who is himself our perfect cornerstone, is the foundation block of our lives, the one upon whom we are built and joined together. In light of this truth, you can see how in the religious leaders' rejection of him (Matt. 21:42), they were choosing to build their own building according to their own plans and how it was inevitable that their building would come crashing down around them (1 Pet. 2:7–8; Matthew 23).

Our union with Christ is a holy temple built upon and joined to him and in which the Holy Spirit dwells. Filled with the Holy

Spirit, this new temple is alive and growing into a glorious building while it rests in secure relation upon the foundation he has laid through his Word.

## THE LORD'S PRAYER

On the night of his betrayal, the Lord Jesus prayed to his Father, and his prayer is recorded for us in John 17. This prayer gives us insight into the conversation of the Son with the Father, and to say that it is deep, mysterious, and holy is simply a failure to find words that properly describe it. Here we are privy to the way the Son speaks to his Father at the beginning of the most trying time of his life. (Although study of this holy prayer could occupy our mind for years, we're only going to look at one portion of it. Let me encourage you to read it in its entirety in appendix 3.) What follows is the portion of the prayer that speaks particularly of our oneness with Christ:

> I in them and you in me, that they may become perfectly one, so that the world may know that you sent me and loved them even as you loved me. Father, I desire that they also, whom you have given me, may be with me where I am, to see my glory that you have given me because you loved me before the foundation of the world. O righteous Father, even though the world does not know you, I know you, and these know that you have sent me. I made known to them your name, and I will continue to make it known, that the love with which you have loved me may be in them, and I in them. (John 17:23–26)

Here we see the Son reaffirming his relationship with his Father and talking with him about those who have believed in him through the words of his disciples—us.

And here also we come to another shocking facet of our union with him: not only are we one with him but he is also one with us. Not only do we have that "in-ness" that we considered at the beginning of this chapter—not only are we in him, but (amazing truth!) he is also in us. We are in him, *and* he is in us. Consider his words: "I in them." The depth and mystery of this unity is without a doubt beyond our understanding. Jesus likened it to the depth of unity he has with his Father. The unity the Son has with the Father is the same unity he has with us. He follows his statement, "I in them," with the astounding statement, ". . . and you in me." He compares his union with us to the perfect oneness that exists among the members of the Trinity. Of course, his prayer here is that we might come to understand our unity with one another through our unity in him and he in us, but in our eagerness to try to figure out what we're supposed to be doing, let us not gloss over the deep mystery that he's speaking of: we are in him, and he is in us in the same way that he is in the Father, and the Father is in him.

> On the highest level of being [our oneness] is compared to the union which exists between the persons of the trinity in the Godhead. This is staggering, but it is the case.[4]

Consider how Jesus describes this oneness we have with the Father and Son and they have with us: "If anyone loves me, he will keep my word, and my *Father will love him, and we will come to him and make our home with him*" (John 14:23). God—Father, Son, and Spirit—*actually* lives in us, like you live in your home, if your home were alive and growing. Wonder of wonders!

Further, mystery of mysteries, Jesus rejoices in the love that the Father has for us, his Son's bride. Again, he says that it is analogous to the love that the Father has for him, his beloved Son. I wonder how much our lives would change if we marinated our souls in the truth that the love the Father has for us is the same as the love he has for his Son. Jesus said that the Father had loved him from "before the foundation of the world." So, we, too, have been loved in the same way for that long—since before the foundation of the world. His love is demonstrated in his election of us, "even as he chose us in him before the foundation of the world, that we should be holy and blameless before him" (Eph. 1:4).

The Lord Jesus is in us, and with him comes the love with which the Father has loved us. "I in them." Think of that. This union with him is far beyond anything we've considered so far. This reciprocal oneness is, in fact, exactly what Paul means when he writes about the rich mystery God has revealed to the Gentiles, "which is Christ in you, the hope of glory" (Col. 1:26–27).

> God himself, in the person of Christ, will be directly and personally present in the lives of his people, and his presence assures them of a future life with him when he returns.[5]

This indwelling of Christ within us is something far greater than anything that was known until he came as the incarnate Messiah. In the Old Testament the Lord dwelt among his chosen people, the Jews, but now, the very Son of God dwells in us, in both Jew and Gentile. This indwelling of the Spirit of Christ within us is what gives us hope for our future with him, and here we are, back again at our Lord's prayer. He prayed that we would be with him so that we might "see" his glory and the glory of the Father; indeed we even share in his glory, for the glory that the Father had given to the Son he has given to us (John 17:22). Because Christ is in us, this is our hope:

> But if Christ is in you, although the body is dead because of sin, the Spirit is life because of righteousness. If the Spirit of him who raised Jesus from the dead dwells in you, he who raised Christ Jesus from the dead will also give life to your mortal bodies through his Spirit who dwells in you. (Rom. 8:10–11)

In sum, all the blessings that have been bestowed upon us are because we are in him and because he is in us. Because he died and rose again, we too have died with him and are raised again. That same Spirit that resurrected his physical body will also resurrect ours, because he dwells in us.

We're walking into the Most Holy Place in communion with the triune God. We've been raised up and made to sit together in heaven in Christ Jesus (Eph. 2:6). We are encouraged to draw near to him "in full assurance of faith" (Heb. 10:22) for the simple reason that we do not approach God's throne alone but in the one who is already there, representing us. Isn't this study of our "one witness" in Christ amazing? And here's yet another way to look at it.

## ADOPTED SONS (AND DAUGHTERS)

Another rich analogy that describes our union with Christ is that of adoption. As you know, adoption is a legal process whereby one person chooses to receive another person into his family and gives to that person all the privileges and advantages of the adopting family while placing upon that family every obligation that the adopted one brings with him.

In the case of our union with Christ, God has chosen to take upon himself all of our debt and obligation. Every expression of adoration and every act of obedience that we are obligated to offer to him, he has performed for us. In addition, every censure and punishment that we earned for failing to worship and obey, he has placed upon his Son. Because we are his adopted sons, we have all the rights of the other Son in the house who has borne all the wrath we deserve and earned all the inheritance we receive.

John speaks of our rights as adopted children in connection with the faith that God has willed to bestow upon us:

> But to all who did receive him, who believed in his name, he gave the right to become children of God, who were born, not of blood nor of the will of the flesh nor of the will of man, but of God. (John 1:12–13)[6]

Upon his return to heaven, the Son sent his Holy Spirit to the church, a gift that our standing as his children gave us a right to inherit. In that one action, he made us one with himself, binding us together with him in one Spirit.

Part of the work of the Spirit in our lives is to convince us of the astounding truths of our union with Christ, that we really are

God's children and that we really are qualified to inherit all his treasures. We are no longer to live as fearful slaves, because our relationship with God has changed. He is no longer our just judge. He is our loving Father, who bestows good gifts on us.

Now we now have a new identity—that of God's children. We have been "filled with the Spirit, united to Christ, and given access to the Father in God's household."[7] He is the Lord, the King "and he desires for us to be his adopted children."[8] This is what the Spirit teaches us when he gives us faith to address God as our Father in the dearest terms:

> For you did not receive the spirit of slavery to fall back into fear, but you have received the Spirit of adoption as sons, by whom we cry, "Abba! Father!" The Spirit himself bears witness with our spirit that we are children of God, and if children, then heirs—heirs of God and fellow heirs of Christ. (Rom. 8:15–17)

Are you struggling to believe? Call out to your Daddy! Are you confused or tempted? Are you sinking beneath a load of sin? Call your Father. Don't be afraid that approaching him in this way is presumptuous or will anger or disappoint him. It doesn't matter what your relationship with your earthly father might have been like. This Father is different, and he's gone so far as to share with you his Spirit—part of his own being—so that you will be assured that your cries are welcome and will always be heard and answered.

## THE SON'S INHERITANCE

The Spirit also tells us that, as sons, we have an inheritance awaiting us. It is the inheritance that Christ earned for us in fulfilling every part of his Father's will. This inheritance is made up of every blessing his perfect filial obedience merited. Everything that is his is now ours, for "all are yours, and you are Christ's, and Christ is God's" (1 Cor. 3:22–23). In addition, since we belong to Jesus, then we are "Abraham's offspring" and "heirs according to promise" (Gal. 3:29). What is this promised inheritance?

I will make of you a great nation, and I will bless you and make your name great, so that you will be a blessing. I will bless those who bless you, and him who dishonors you I will curse, and in you all the families of the earth shall be blessed. (Gen. 12:2–3)

What an inheritance! It is no wonder we need a supernatural work of the Holy Spirit to believe it. We need him to help us believe that these words, spoken so many years ago over Abraham, are actually words of promise to God's Son and, by his work and our adoption, spoken to us. We are not alone. We are a great nation. We are no longer cursed or in exile. In fact, not only do we have a blessing; we *are* a blessing. God will protect and care for us as part of his global, universal, and forever family, and because of the work he has ordained that we should do (Eph. 2:10), we will be a source of blessing to many other families. Does that seem hard to believe? Of course it does. But Jesus knows your weaknesses, and he has sent his Spirit to help you. Ask him for help now.

How could he adopt us? How is it that we have the rights and privileges of obedient sons? You know that answer by now, don't you? "You are no longer a slave, but a son, and if a son, then an heir through God." It happened because "God sent forth his Son" (Gal. 4:4–7). Jesus was born of a woman (one of us). He was born under the law like us, having to obey it in order to merit God's favor. And he did. It is because of his work that we have received adoption as sons.

## HOW NEEDFUL IS OUR UNION

I know we've covered a lot in this chapter, and I know how mysterious this union with Christ is, but, oh, how impoverished our souls are when we neglect this sweet doctrine. How alone, how weak, and how lost we feel when we are ignorant of it. Yet it is an ocean so deep, so full, we can't even begin to skim across its surface without the help of the Spirit, and even then in starts and stumbles. Do you feel overwhelmed? Me too. Thank God for the Spirit and that he will make known to us all we need to know today.

## FOUND IN HIM

1) We have considered our union with Christ in this chapter in several ways. Consider what is precious to you about each one and write out your responses here:

    a) We are dead to sin and alive to God:
    b) We have eternal life:
    c) We have freedom from condemnation:
    d) We are freed from the principle of sin and death:
    e) We can be assured that we have the love of God:
    f) We are his temple, a living building:

2) What is it about the Lord's prayer in John 17, his being *in us*, that is especially meaningful to you? Why?

3) What is it about our adoption and inheritance that is especially meaningful to you? Why?

4) Why is Christ's gift of the Holy Spirit precious to you in light of your union with him?

5) Consider the words of the following hymn and rejoice:

> Dear Saviour, I am Thine,
> By everlasting bands,
> My name, my heart, I would resign;
> My soul is in Thy hands.
>
> To Thee I still would cleave
> With ever-growing zeal;
> If millions tempt me Christ to leave,
> They never shall prevail.
>
> His Spirit shall unite
> My soul to Him, my Head;
> Shall form me to His image bright,
> And teach His path to tread.
>
> Death may my soul divide

From this abode of clay;
But love shall keep me near Thy side
Through all the gloomy way.
Since Christ and we are one,
Why should we doubt or fear?
If He in heaven hath fix'd His throne,
He'll fix His members there.[9]

6) Summarize in four or five sentences what you have learned in this chapter.

# 8

# He Gave Himself
# Up for Us

*Christ loved the church and gave himself up for her.*

EPHESIANS 5:25

The glorious incarnation that we've been considering means that we will never be alone, never separated from God. We are one with him through the union of Jesus's two natures: he has united God and man together into one new man, Jesus Christ. Jesus could no more dissolve his union with humanity than he could sever his deity from the human body he has taken to himself. There is simply no way to overestimate the eternal covenant he has made to be one with us. But, as we've begun to discover, the incarnation is not the only way in which we are one with him.

## ONE WITH HIM IN MARRIAGE

Our oneness with Jesus is spoken of in many ways in the Bible: a vine and branches (John 15:1–10), a building and foundation (Eph. 2:19–21), and a body with its members (1 Cor. 12:12). But each of these images is only a metaphor meant to help us understand the reality, which is our marriage with him. *In eternity we will not be branches or buildings or a body. We will be a bride.* Marriage with him is more than a metaphor; it is the reality that all the other metaphors describe.

Paul gets at this truth when he gives instructions to husbands in a familiar passage from Ephesians 5. To help glean the truth about Jesus's love and purpose for us as his bride from these verses, I've paraphrased the passage so that the focus will be on his work rather than on ours. You'll notice that I've removed the commands to husbands and left only the descriptions of Jesus's work.[1] I believe that this is a legitimate use of this passage, for at the end of it Paul himself writes that his instructions to husbands actually refer to Christ and the church:

> Christ loved the church and gave himself up for her, that he might sanctify her, having cleansed her by the washing of water with the word, so that he might present the church to himself in splendor, without spot or wrinkle or any such thing, that she might be holy and without blemish. [He has loved her as he loved his own body, and because he is one with her, when he is loving her, he is loving himself.] Jesus never hated his own flesh, but nourishes and cherishes it, just as Christ does the church, because we are members of his body. "Therefore a man shall leave his father and mother and hold fast to his wife, and the two shall become one flesh." This mystery is profound, and I am saying that it refers to Christ and the church. (Eph. 5:25–32)

At the outset, let's just admit that these truths are a profound mystery to us. How can the millions of believers who make up the church be united in marriage with God, who is also man, while we're here on earth and he is there in heaven? We echo Paul's thought: this is a profound mystery. So let's begin our quest for understanding with humility by saying that although we will delve into the dark, asking God for light, we won't be able to completely see it all. There are some things that will simply remain a mystery to us—at least for now. We can be assured, however, that he will give us illumination to understand everything we need to know for today.

Our passage begins in this way: "Christ loved the church and gave himself up for her." Everything we've seen so far has demonstrated his self-sacrificing love. He grieved over his poor bride's plight, so in love he gave of himself to relieve her suffering. She was lost, alone, alienated from God, under condemnation, and without hope. As a loving groom, he grieved over her troubles. He never said, "You've made your bed, now sleep in it." No, he gave. He gave himself. He gave up the freedom he had as a spirit to be eternally clothed in human flesh. He gave up his prerogative to rule as king and lay down his life to become a servant. And he gave up his relationship with his Father when he took upon himself all the rejection and alienation we deserve. He gave himself up for the one he loves.

## A BEAUTIFUL BRIDE

Why would he give like this? He gave so that he might have a beautiful bride. He gave so that he might beautify his bride, presenting her to himself without any sin—no spot, wrinkle, or blemish. His self-giving transforms her from filthy rebel into a bride described by the word "splendor." He gave this beautiful bride to himself by cleansing her through washing with the word of the gospel—life transforming words about his work on our behalf that sanctify and purify us. His whole goal was to make us fit for him, a glorious queen fit for a king.

Oh, how different this groom is! So many men look for a woman who is already beautiful—one who will enhance their resume and make other men think that they have value. Jesus did just the opposite. He went and found the most vile creature he could and set about beautifying her by taking her vileness upon himself and fully identifying with her, thereby remaking her into his image. Yes, eventually this does accrue to his glory, but it's not how most men look to advance themselves.

In loving her, he actually loved his own body, for he had taken her form to himself and loved her because she was, through the incarnation, just like him. He became one of her own kind, one of her race, one of her flesh. Paul writes that "no one ever hated his own flesh," and when you make these words about Christ instead of human husbands, the truth becomes so dear. He did not hate taking our flesh upon himself, nor will he ever hate or look down upon us because we are mere flesh and blood. Instead he loves, nourishes, and cherishes us because he is just like us.

## HE NOURISHES AND CHERISHES US

Jesus accomplished our union first of all through his physical body, which is the true bread that came down out of heaven. This is the bread we must eat, the bread that gives life to the world (John 6:33). He also shed his blood, which is the true drink we imbibe, poured out and transfused into our bodies and without which we have no life. His description of our oneness with him should set us back on our heels: "Whoever feeds on my flesh and drinks my blood abides in me, and I in him. . . . Whoever feeds on me . . . will live because of me. . . . Whoever feeds on this bread will live forever." Profound mystery? Yes. In response to this mystery even his disciples said, "This is a hard saying." Our only hope of understanding is that "it is the Spirit who gives life" (vv. 56–63). Our natural reasoning is of no help at all. Again, let us in humility pray that the Lord would illumine our minds to these things.

Right now Jesus is nourishing and cherishing us by the Spirit through his graces to the church—through the word of the gospel, through the Word preached and the sacraments given. As a faithful husband, he has never neglected his duty to provide all that his bride needs to be the glorious woman he desires.

Further, in fulfilling his role as the second Adam, Jesus left his father and mother to cleave unto his wife. He left his Father when he left Father's throne in heaven, and he left his mother when, on the cross, he gave her into John's keeping (John 19:26). Leaving Father and mother, he then cleaved to his wife when, by the blood and water that poured from his heart, the church was born and given to him so that the God-man and his wife became one. Since that moment he has "held fast" to her, and he will *never* let her go. How could he? We are one!

Again, Jesus is the second Adam, and we are his bride, bone of his bones and flesh of his flesh. We are now "one flesh" with him not only because of the incarnation (his taking to himself our flesh) but also because we are married to him. We are one with him just as a husband and wife are one. This oneness is not a physical union but rather a spiritual one, a covenant relationship in which he has bound himself to us in indissoluble union forever. We are "joined to the Lord" and have become "one spirit with him" (1 Cor. 6:17).

The covenant relationship we have with our heavenly husband cannot ever be severed any more than his human body could be torn from his nature as the Word. He has made covenant vows and entered into a binding relationship with us. He spoke those vows over us when he promised that he would betroth us to himself and that we would know him intimately. In essence, at his darkest moment in Gethsemane, when by the strength of his love and in the power of the Spirit he said, "Thy will be done," he was looking at us and saying, "I do." And along with his vow he has also gifted us with faith to respond "I do" to his wooing. Marriage vows have been spoken. We are united to him forever. Paul even goes so far as to say that we have been joined to "him who was raised from the dead." Our joining with him, though not physical, is real, for it even results in reproduction of children, "that we may bear fruit for God" (Rom. 7:4). We are "legally and organically one" with him in marriage, right now.[2]

The Lord Jesus purposed to have a bride, and he chose you individually to be part of the church corporately. He bought her and brought her to himself at great cost. The Lord Jesus and his bride, the church, have been joined together by God himself, so that we are no longer two, but one. No man, and especially not *the* faithful man, Christ Jesus, will ever separate us. He will never leave us nor forsake us (Heb. 13:5). Nothing can separate us from the love God has for us (Rom. 8:38–39). He will never divorce us for having found some "indecency" in us (Deut. 24:1). After all, he knew all of our indecencies before he ever committed to marrying us, and because of his work, he has beautified us so that all our degradation is gone. He will never treat us "treacherously," throwing us aside for some newer model as Israel's husbands had (Mal. 2:14 NASB). We are Christ's trophy wife now.

When John looked into heaven, he saw a future marriage feast and the Lamb with his bride who had made herself ready (Rev. 19:7). John saw this celebration as though it had already occurred in time. Remember that in the ancient Near East a promise of betrothal or engagement was as significant as the actual marriage ceremony—which is why Joseph initially thought he would "divorce" or "put away" Mary for her supposed infidelity, although they had not actually been married yet. We too are betrothed to Christ, and that betrothal is as significant a change in our marital status as if an actual wedding had occurred. That's how assured we can be of his commitment to us; in God's sight our marriage has *already* happened.

## TRANSPARENT, TRUSTWORTHY LOVE

In the meantime, it is before him now that we can nakedly and unashamedly stand. Because he hung there, naked and exposed before every eye, bearing our shame, we now can stand transparently and without any fig-leaf disguises to try to hide our failures or make us more presentable to him. We don't need to do that; he's seen it all, he knows it all, and he's borne it all. We can be completely at ease and rest in his bosom. There isn't anything we can say or do that will shock him or cause him to break his vow to faithfully love and stand by us. He'll never send us away; we'll always be found in him.

There isn't a person reading this now who hasn't experienced rejection and desertion in some way. My father and mother divorced when I was quite young, and I'm very familiar with the feelings of rejection and desertion that come from being part of a broken family. But whether or not you grew up in a single-parent family, we all know what it is like to trust the untrustworthy. And that's not all: each of us, in one way or another, has failed to keep our word as we should. We have made promises we haven't kept. We, too, have been untrustworthy. We all share this common bond of disappointment and broken relationships. But that's not what union with Christ is like, for Jesus, our heavenly groom, is completely trustworthy. We can be assured of that because of all he's done to prove himself to us; from the incarnation to the crucifixion to the resurrection, he's shown himself completely worthy of our faith. When he says, "I won't leave you," we can rest our souls on that truth forever. "There is no communion among men that is comparable to fellowship with Christ—he communes with his people and his people commune with him in conscious reciprocal love."[3]

## NO FOREIGN WIVES!

Throughout biblical history the Lord commanded his people to refrain from marrying those who were not part of his covenant. Both Old and New Testaments limit whom a believer may marry to those who are "in the Lord" (Deut. 7:3; Ezra 9:2; 1 Cor. 7:39; see also 2 Cor. 6:14). In fact, it was such a great abomination to the Lord for God's holy people to intermarry with the pagan nations around them that when the exiles returned to Jerusalem from Babylon, they were actually commanded to divorce their "foreign" wives. A mixed marriage is monstrous to the Lord. God's holy children are never to intermingle with the unholy.

How could it be, then, that the Father would give the holy Son of God in marriage to an apostate, pagan bride? How could he take to his own bosom the children of disobedience upon whom the wrath of his Father lay? How could he violate his own command and marry us? *Only through the atonement the Son would bring, an atonement that opened the door for him to marry sinners.*

## AT ONE WITH HIM

Historically, the word *atonement* has been defined as the "at-one-ment," or the reconciliation between God and man. Because we have, by thought, word, and deed, broken the Father's commands, the original loving, familial relationship mankind had with God was shattered. Outside of Christ, we were anything but "one flesh" with him. Rather than enjoying marital love, our relationship with him was characterized by guilt on our side and impending punishment on his. Our relationship with God was infused with guilt and wrath; he was not our loving Father but rather our just judge.

In the atonement, however, Jesus Christ expiated our guilt and propitiated our punishment. Let me explain what that means. Through his life and death, Jesus cleansed our sin and cancelled the record of wrongdoing that stood against us. This record "he set aside, nailing it to the cross" (Col. 2:14). He also forgave us all our sins and propitiated or bore away all the wrath that hung over our heads. Because he had no sin of his own, he was qualified to pay the penalty for ours, thereby opening the door for the forgiveness the Father longed to grant (Ps. 86:5).

In addition, because Jesus bore away all of God's wrath for all of our sin, his Father no longer looked at us as undesirable, indecent women but rather as beloved daughters who would, of course, be welcomed into his family through marriage. Because of the atonement, our relationship with God is reconciled. Jesus paid the price that was demanded by his Father for our sin. He redeemed us. The Father insisted that the Son wed a perfect bride, and he has, and we are the perfect bride.

The work of the Lord Jesus enabled him to wed us without his violating the command against marrying foreign wives. He has made us one with him and also with each other:

> Remember that you were at that time separated from Christ, alienated . . . and strangers to the covenants of promise, having no hope and without God in the world. But now in Christ Jesus you who once were far off have been brought near by the blood

of Christ. . . . And he came and preached peace to you who were
far off and peace to those who were near. (Eph. 2:12–13, 17)

We are no longer strangers and aliens. He can marry us. Both
the apostate Jew (who refused him) and the Jew's enemy, the Gentile, who was busy constructing idols, are now qualified to wed the
Son of God. Jesus Christ has atoned for our sins and unified us as
one pure virgin (2 Cor. 11:2). He too is a pure virgin, our kinsman-
redeemer, our dear Boaz, who isn't ashamed to take us, a Moabite
widow, into his home (see Ruth 4:13).

## AN OFFERING BY THE GOD-MAN

Our Lord Jesus has united us with the Father, making atonement
for us by the offering of his lifeblood. Because he wanted us to be
his bride, he had to die in our place as the God-man. He had to die
as a sinless human so that he could fully represent us as the sinless second Adam. In this way the incarnation and the cross went
hand in hand to accomplish our atonement. That soft baby lying
sweetly in a feeding trough with human blood flowing through his
little veins had only one purpose: to bring reconciliation between
his Father and his bride (including Mary, his earthly mother) by
pouring out his blood in offering in their place to atone for their
sin. There was simply no other avenue for God to reconcile himself to us, to be just and justifier of those who have faith in him
(Rom. 3:26).

But our groom, the eternal Son of God, became a man so that
he could die for us (Heb. 2:14–15). God cannot die, but the one
who died for us was God. As the God-man he bore the punishment
that was due us, a punishment infinite in scope that only divin-
ity could bear. We would have borne God's unmitigated wrath for
eternity. There never would have been a time when God would
have looked at us in our torment and said, "Okay, that's enough."
So all that punishment had to be meted out upon him on the
cross. Only God himself could bear up under this infinite penalty.
In addition, only the God-man's suffering was of such value and

intensity that just six hours of it was equal to an eternity's worth of suffering for all of us. Our heavenly husband had to be both God and man in order to atone for our sins, and the suffering he endured is beyond imagination.

## AN OFFERING OF THE BLOOD OF LIFE

The sacrificial system of sin offerings found in the Old Testament was for the purpose of Israel's temporary atonement. Specific offerings, bulls and goats, were to be made for the people's "unintentional sins," whereby the blood of the animal slaughtered would cover the guilt of sin. When the Bible speaks of the blood of a sacrificed animal being offered, that blood symbolizes the actual life of the animal, which had to be offered in the place of the sinner who deserved death. Here are two passages, one from the Old Testament and one from the New Testament, about the necessity of the shedding of blood or, in other words, the sacrificing of a life to atone for sin:

> For the life of the flesh is in the blood, and I have given it for you on the altar to make atonement for your souls, for it is the blood that makes atonement by the life. (Lev. 17:11)

> Indeed, under the law almost everything is purified with blood, and without the shedding of blood there is no forgiveness of sins. (Heb. 9:22)

Here's the shocking reality: the entire sacrificial system of the Old Testament was simply a foreshadowing of the "good things to come," the sacrifice made on the cross of Christ. Animal blood was never meant to be a permanent solution to anyone's sin problem. The writer to the Hebrews tells us that we can be sure of this because the Old Testament sacrificial system was flawed from the outset. For instance, the sacrifices had to be offered continually, year by year, and not just for the sins of the people but also for the sins of the priests themselves. Year after year animals screamed in terror and blood poured out upon the ground. Up onto the flaming brazen altar the carcasses of animals were thrown to burn to ash so that by blood and smoke God's wrath would be temporarily appeased and the unintentional sins of the people would be covered.

Everyday the priests themselves were swathed in blood and reeked of burning flesh. On and on these sacrifices went, and still there was no sacrifice sufficient to remove sin and guilt and perfect the worshiper because "it is impossible for the blood of bulls and goats to take away sins" (Heb. 10:4). *Until the incarnation and the cross!* For Jesus, our Great High Priest, offered himself as the final sacrifice for sins. For by that "single offering he has *perfected for all time* those who are being sanctified" by it (vv. 12, 14). Do you see the infinite value of the God-man's sacrifice? By this *single offering* he has perfected us for all time. Our sins are no longer simply covered over. No! They are completely wiped away—not just our "unintentional sins" but all our sins; and not just the sins we committed before we came to faith but all the sins we've committed since then and (get ready now) all the sins we have yet to commit. He's made a single offering. His offering was of such value that he has perfected us for all time. That's how infinitely costly and profoundly excruciating his suffering for us was.

The price he paid to perfect us, to make us fit to marry him, to ransom us and ensure our union with him, was not some measly dowry or bride-price. No, it was "not with perishable things such as silver or gold, but with the precious blood of Christ, like that of a lamb without blemish or spot" (1 Pet. 1:18–19). What precious blood! What priceless treasure was in each drop that fell from his dying body! It was blood from a life that was valuable enough to ransom us all. His bloody death was sufficient to completely wash away all our guilt before a holy God who is aware of what we really are. By the shed blood of the sinless Lamb, all of our guilt for sin has been erased so that we are now reconciled (or "at one") with God.

Again, Jesus knew exactly why he had been given a body and what it would take to redeem us and make us his bride. He said that he had come not like a great lord to exercise authority over his bride—he could, after all, demand that she submit to his rule and force her to bow her knee—but rather he came as a servant, to "give his life as a ransom" (Mark 10:45) and pour out his covenant blood for her (14:24).

> All this is from God, who through Christ reconciled us to himself ... that is, in Christ God was reconciling the world to himself, not counting their trespasses against them. (2 Cor. 5:18–19)

Oh, amazing grace! The atonement removes the barrier of our sinful record and establishes our covenant relationship with him in marriage, but this union with him goes even farther.

## ONE HEAD, ONE BODY

In considering our oneness or union with Christ, we've been drawing a lot of analogies from the Genesis story in the garden of Eden. He's another one for us to consider.

At first, before the creation of Eve, Adam lived alone in the garden. The Bible tells us that although all his physical needs were completely satisfied, his aloneness wasn't good. In fact, the original language there is stronger than "it's okay for him to be alone, but it's not the best." The Hebrew tells us concerning his aloneness that "it's positively bad."[4] Adam's aloneness was positively bad because God so loves fellowship between persons that he exists in the Trinity, and because we have been created in his image, we too are meant to live in communal union, or communion and fellowship, too.

After looking at all the animals, Adam realized that there was nothing like him; no part of the animal world "imaged" God as he did. So the Lord anesthetized him and took out of his side flesh and bone, which he then fashioned into one who was like him, but different. God made Eve for Adam (Gen. 2:20–22). In this process Adam was split into two in such a way that without his counterpart, woman, he would never be whole again.[5] Just as God's answer to Adam's aloneness was Eve, his answer to the man Jesus's aloneness is the church.[6] In the same way that the husband is one with and the head of the wife in a human marriage, so Jesus now is the head of the church, his body, of whom he is Savior (Eph. 5:23).

Paul's writings are filled with union language and especially with this "Christ as head, the church as body" motif. For instance, "He put all things under his feet and gave him as head over all things to the church, which is his body, the fullness of him who fills all in all" (Eph. 1:22–23).

Jesus has so "identified himself with his church that it is said to be his very body."[7] He is permanently in union with her in the same way that your head is permanently in union with your physical body. It is impossible now that your head and body have been joined for one to survive without the other. Jesus's union with us is not mere metaphor. No, it is living reality. Yes, there are many parts of our bodies—we have arms, legs, and eyes. There are many members in our body, but the body is still only one. So it is with our union with Jesus, "for just as the body is one and has many members, and all the members of the body, though many, are one body, *so it is with Christ* (1 Cor. 12:12).

Notice the "now-ness" of this living union: "*Now* you are the body of Christ and individually members of it" (1 Cor. 12:27). Our union with him isn't something that will begin when we're in heaven or when he returns to earth. No, right now, at this moment, we are in union with him.

Further, this *now* union with him doesn't involve only our spirits or our souls. No, Paul actually says that our bodies are already "members" or parts of the body "of Christ" (1 Cor. 6:15). Think of that! Your physical body, as you're sitting here reading this book, is actually part of Christ's body. You, in every part of who you are, in your spirit, soul, *and* body, are one with him.

At this point you might be thinking: *Okay, I'm beginning to un-*

derstand that I am one with Christ, but how does that work? I mean, I am here on earth, and he is there in heaven. How can we actually be one when we're divided by such a great distance and by such dissimilarity in status?

As he promised, at his ascension Jesus sent the Holy Spirit down upon his body, the church. The Spirit that he sent is the very Spirit who indwelt him at his conception and his baptism. It is the same Spirit that raised him from the dead. And it is that same Spirit that he now shares with us (1 John 4:13). While we cannot see the Spirit with our eyes, we can be fully assured that our union with him is just as real as if we could.

## ONE IN MARRIAGE

I've been married now for nearly forty years. I can hardly believe that Phil and I have been together that long! Back in 1974 we spoke covenant vows in front of our families and friends and made promises to the Lord that we would honor our union together and that it would be paramount in our lives. By his grace, the Lord has enabled us to stay together, and the union, although there at the beginning of our marriage, has become more and more evident to us both as the years have passed. In other words, the union we had by virtue of our vows in 1974 is the same union we have now; it's just that we're more aware of what that union means, since we've been together for so long.

A significant part of what the Lord has called me to do involves extensive travel. For instance, in 2013 it's my plan (Lord willing) to travel to more than twenty events across the country. During this travel time, Phil and I will probably be separated. But this separation, sometimes by thousands of miles, does not interrupt the union or oneness that we have. While I'm gone, even though we're not together in the same house, we talk frequently; but even if we didn't, the oneness of our marriage wouldn't change.

In the same way, the oneness we have with Jesus through the unity given by the Spirit doesn't change just because Jesus is seated at the right hand of his Father and we are still on earth.

In fact, the union we have with him is far greater than what Phil and I have, because Phil and I will one day be separated through death, and our oneness will be broken (a fact proven by a widow or widower's right to remarry). But we will never be separated from Jesus. Because he has already died and we are one with him, death will never separate us again.

## ONE IN THE MILITARY

Here's one more example. A man or a woman who has joined the armed forces of my country is a member of a body of people who are spread out all over the globe. No matter where they are posted, they are in union, or one with, other US servicemen and women. On a day-to-day basis they serve alongside those in their particular company, but they are one even with those with whom they do not serve side by side. Every one of them has taken vows to follow the direction of their head, the president of the United States, as he makes his will known through generals and company commanders.

While it is probably true that none of them will ever meet the president face-to-face or ever hear his voice speaking to them personally, they still know that he is their head and that they are the body that he is using to accomplish his goals.

Can you see how it is the same way with you and your Lord? He is the head of a body, and the union between that head and body are just as real (more real!) than the unity between your head and body, between you and your spouse (if you are married), and between a soldier and his commander-in-chief.

## MARRIAGE AND ATONEMENT

I know that I've given you a lot to think about in this chapter, so let's just take a moment to review what our union with Christ means.

To begin with, we talked about our marriage to Jesus and all that he had to do to qualify us to be his bride. Let me encourage you to allow these truths to warm your affections for him today. The work that he did to purchase you for himself should speak to you about his commitment to continue to love you, no matter how you fail, and should assure your heart that you are forever his. Your husband or wife, mother or father, or friends or acquaintances may forsake you, but he never will. Once he said "I do"—something he first uttered before the foundation of the world and sealed in blood on the cross—for him that meant an eternal commitment that can never be violated.

> I give [my sheep] eternal life, and they will never perish, and no one will snatch them out of my hand. My Father, who has given them to me, is greater than all, and no one is able to snatch them out of the Father's hand. (John 10:28–29)

> Who shall separate us from the love of Christ? Shall tribulation, or distress, or persecution, or famine, or nakedness, or danger, or sword? As it is written, "For your sake we are being killed all the day long; we are regarded as sheep to be slaughtered." . . . For I am sure that [nothing] in all creation will be able to separate us from the love of God in Christ Jesus our Lord. (Rom. 8:35–36, 38–39)

It is Jesus, who stands at an altar united with his bride, who is holding onto us. He has his arms around us. Do you think anyone (including you) could break his grip? He experienced tribulation, distress, persecution, famine, nakedness, danger, and sword. It was for our sake that he was a lamb to be slaughtered. In light of this, do you honestly think that there is anything that can separate you from the love of God in Christ Jesus, who right now is ruling as a human king from heaven?

We also discussed that atonement means that we are "at one" now with God and how Jesus Christ did all the work necessary to accomplish this. He offered his life, his body, and his blood to perfect us forever so that in his sight we are beautiful, pure virgins, splendid brides qualified to be his wife. By his one sacrifice he has perfected you *forever*!

Right now, as you sit here reading this book, you are as one with him as you will ever be. Of course, when you die and your faith becomes sight, you will understand this profound mystery more clearly, but the reality of it will not have changed. Rejoice.

## FOUND IN HIM

1) "We also rejoice in God through our Lord Jesus Christ, through whom we now have received reconciliation" (Rom. 5:11). How often do you rejoice because of the reconciliation? What would "rejoicing in God" look like in your life?

2) We are united, one with him for "the bodies of Christians are one with the resurrected Christ."[8] Although this is a great mystery, ask the Holy Spirit to help you understand. How would your life be different if you really believed that you were one like this with the resurrected Christ?

3) "The eternal Son became our brother; took upon Himself our sin . . . paid our debt to the majesty of [unbreakable] law; covered our nakedness with His righteousness; presented us, as those in whose stead He appeared, unblamable and acceptable to the Father; excited the hallelujahs of angels at our exaltation; elevated us to a participation of His own riches, blessedness, and privileges; pitched tents of peace for us around the throne of God; and connected us with Himself by the bonds of eternal gratitude and affection. Such is the edifice which the Almighty reared upon the ruins of sin."[9] Respond.

4) Summarize what you've learned in this chapter in four or five sentences.

# Chosen, Betrothed, Beloved, and Named

*For your Maker is your husband,*
*the LORD of hosts is his name;*
*and the Holy One of Israel is your Redeemer. . . .*
*For the LORD has called you*
*like a wife deserted and grieved in spirit, . . .*
*but with everlasting love I will have compassion on you.*

ISAIAH 54:5–6, 8

Consider again those words above from Isaiah. Your maker, the Word made flesh, your redeemer, is your husband. Your husband. Yes, I know we've already spent a significant amount of time considering this topic, but we're going back there again. Guys, I know that this might be an uncomfortable concept for you, but that's what the Bible says. You are a beloved bride.

Perhaps any struggle you're having with this metaphor will be helped by something C. S. Lewis said. The truth is that in Christ, we must all think of ourselves as feminine, as followers, not initiators; as receivers, as in a subordinate position. C. S. Lewis described the femininity of us all (men and women) when he wrote that in comparison to God, we're all feminine. "What is above and beyond all things is so masculine that we are all feminine in relation to it."[1] God himself is the archetype of masculinity, and every way that we think about true masculinity flows from the nature of who he is. He is what it means to be masculine, and everything else, even the most burly of men, falls far short of it. So, my brothers, we're going to talk about marriage and your being a bride some more, but don't get nervous. Whenever anyone got around Jesus they felt both welcomed and in need of protection and provision, and they all came to know that he had initiated the relationship and was completely in charge. Well, if they didn't know it at first, they eventually did.

Not only would those near him know that he was the head, the leader, the masculine component of the relationship; they would also know something of even greater significance: they would know that they were loved. There is no imagery that expresses the great love that God has for his people like that of a marriage. Remember, although there are a lot of metaphors for our union with Christ given in the New Testament, only one of them carries over into eternity. We will be his bride forever.

## WE ARE THE CHOSEN

"For we know, brothers and sisters loved by God, that he has chosen you" (1 Thess. 1:4 NIV; see also 2 Thess. 2:13). We can be certain of the Father's love for us from "before the foundation of the world" because we have been given faith to believe that we have been called. If you believe that God's Word is true, that he loves you and desires relationship with you through marriage to his Son, then you are loved by him and part of those "called" to be saints. Paul refers frequently and in tandem to the twin truths of being loved and being called, for example, all those "who are loved by God" are "called to be saints" (Rom. 1:7).

The "chosen-ness," selection, or election that we share as believers is an expression of the Father's love for us. He has called us to be his own. This calling is his "antecedent sovereign act of appointing people for eternal life."[2] In other words, in eternity past, God the Father chose a bride for his Son: specific people for whose sins the Son would die and into whose hearts would be placed the faith to believe and turn toward him.

We don't know why God has chosen us. I don't know why he's chosen me to be his—I wouldn't have. When choosing a bride for a favored son, a father in the ancient Near East would consider the prospects available and pick out the most beautiful, demure, intelligent, godly woman available. He would pick out a woman who would be a faithful wife and a good mother, one who would enhance his son's reputation. But that's not how our heavenly Father chose. No, Isaiah describes the kind of woman the Father has called. She is "like a wife deserted and grieved in spirit" (Isa. 54:6). She's a divorcee. That's the kind of woman he picked for his Son, a woman who would be anything but what we'd expect. Isaiah describes her as a woman who has a checkered history and she has this history not because she's primarily a victim of other's actions against her but because she's turned her back on her Lord. Here are Isaiah's precious words in context of the kind of bride we are:

"For your Maker is your husband,
    the Lord of hosts is his name;
and the Holy One of Israel is your Redeemer,
    the God of the whole earth he is called.
For the Lord has called you
    like a wife deserted and grieved in spirit,
like a wife of youth when she is cast off,
    says your God.
For a brief moment I deserted you,
    but with great compassion I will gather you.
In overflowing anger for a moment
    I hid my face from you,
but with everlasting love I will have compassion on you,"
    says the Lord, your Redeemer. (Isa. 54:5–8)

Notice how we are described: deserted, grieved, cast off. But notice that although this bride is suffering, her wounds are self-inflicted. Yes, she is deserted and cast off, but she's brought this upon herself by turning away from the Lord, her husband, and toward other gods. Consider again how the Lord responds: "With everlasting love I will have compassion on you." What do we deserve? His rejection, his censure. What do we get? His everlasting love and compassion. He calls us to himself that he may bind himself to us in union forever. God's love for his elect always eventuates in their receiving faith that will save them.[3] Why us? Why you, why me? I don't know. I don't know that we'll ever know, but when we're with him in heaven, bound to our husband for eternity, it will be enough.

## WE ARE THE BETROTHED

God the Father has chosen the church to be his Son's bride. Much like the tradition that we still carry on, in the ancient Near East the father of the bride would give his daughter in marriage to the bridegroom. Interestingly, the apostle Paul thought of himself as the father of the church of Corinth and gave her as a pure bride to her husband, Christ (2 Cor. 11:2–3). For Paul, a pure bride was one marked by a pure and simple devotion. This pure and simple devotion that Paul was concerned about was not sinlessness per se but rather a concern that she not commit spiritual adultery by accepting "another Jesus," "a different Spirit," or "a different gospel" (2 Cor. 11:4). He wanted her to believe that the gospel message of simple faith in Christ was all that she needed; that she didn't need another super-Jesus who didn't suffer and would automatically transform her struggle with sin; that she didn't need another spirit, one who would be more flashy. Paul saw himself facilitating God the Father's role as he longed to present his daughter church to Jesus as a bride with a simple virgin faith, one that had not been polluted by the false religions of works-righteousness, mysticism, or superficial emotionalism.

## THE DOWER

In Israel, but also in more recent times, when a father had arranged a marriage for his son, he would give the son a dower to present to his wife as a gift so that she would know she would be provided for after the marriage in case of his death. In twenty-first-century America, fathers no longer give dowers, but we can understand the practice when we compare it to a life insurance policy that a father might give to his son as a gift for his bride. We might also think of the dower as the opposite of a dowry, a gift brought into the marriage by the bride's family (rather than the husband's) to help the husband set up his new home.

As Christ's bride, we have received a rich dower, for at Jesus's death we have received the fullness of God (John 1:16). It was the sacrifice of the Son that unlocked the dower the Father had reserved for us, for, "though he was rich, yet for your sake he became poor, so that you by his poverty might become rich" (2 Cor. 8:9). When did we receive these rich gifts? At his ascension. His death assured us of the bounty, and at his ascension he received gifts from his Father that he gave to the church, his bride (Eph. 4:8). His ascension is actually the event that insured our provision. He gave to us blessings from on high: wisdom, knowledge, and the gifts of the Spirit (1 Corinthians 12).[4] These are just some instances of the wealth with which the church is dowered. The fruit of the Spirit is also a gift of Christ's Spirit, who causes it to grow in our midst. The unsearchable riches of Christ, immeasurable spiritual wealth (Eph. 3:8), were given to us by Christ upon his ascension; from him are "all things" (Rom. 11:36). He bestows "his riches on all who call on him" (10:12), for he has "delivered us from the domain of darkness and transferred us to the kingdom of his beloved Son, in whom we have redemption, the forgiveness of sins" (Col. 1:13–14).

## THE FATHER'S GIFT OF A BRIDE

The Lord Jesus recognized that the Father had given the church to him, for in John 17 he prayed about it: "I am praying for them . . . *for those whom you have given me*, for they are yours" (v. 9). We are God's gift to his Son. Think of that! For his wedding present, the Father gave us to his beloved Son. Who can comprehend such a thought? And how does the Son respond? With a loving heart that longs to be with us:

> Father, I desire that they also, whom you have given me, may be with me where I am, to see my glory that you have given me because you loved me before the foundation of the world. (John 17:24)

The Lord Jesus is awaiting our arrival and the final consummation of our marriage with him in eternity. There, we will be given the most glorious wedding gift ever given: we will see Christ's glory, and our hearts will burst with joy and praise. Until that moment, we are waiting—but so is he. We will get to see the love the Father has for the Son and the glory that they share together. Words will not suffice for us then but only worship.

Not only does the Father give the bride to the Son; he also keeps her safely for him, much as an earthly father would keep his daughter safe for her wedding day. We are "those who are called, beloved in God the Father and kept for Jesus Christ" (Jude 1). Consider those words again. This is your identity. You are "called," "beloved in God the Father," and "kept for Jesus Christ." This is who you really are.

## WE ARE THE BELOVED

> I will call them My people, who were not My people,
> And her beloved, who was not beloved.
> And it shall come to pass in the place where it was said to them,
> "You are not My people,"
> There they shall be called sons of the living God"
>     (Rom. 9:25–26 NKJV).

The theme of the book of Hosea is Israel's desertion of her husband, the Lord; her disloyalty and harlotry with other gods; and her husband's faithfulness. Through his struggles with his own wife, who was a whore, the prophet Hosea experienced God's agony over his bride Israel and his longing for her to return to him while he continued to love her.

During their marriage, Hosea's wife, Gomer, gave birth to several children; he was told to name one "No Mercy," and another "Not My People." But Hosea was subsequently given a vision of a future day, our day, in which God would betroth his people to him forever "in steadfast love and in mercy" (Hos. 2:19–20). This is how Hosea describes God's love for his bride:

> Therefore, behold, I will allure her,
> and bring her into the wilderness,
> and speak tenderly to her.
> And there I will give her her vineyards
> and make the Valley of Achor [trouble] a door of hope. . . .

> And in that day, declares the LORD, you will call me "My Husband" and no longer will you call me "My Baal." . . . And I will betroth you to me forever. I will betroth you to me in righteousness and in justice, in steadfast love and in mercy. I will betroth you to me in faithfulness. And you shall know the LORD (Hos. 2:14–16, 19–20).

On the day when the Lord will "atone for you for all that you have done" (Ezek. 16:63), he will change the name of our accursed children. Upon "No Mercy" will his mercy rest, and "Not My People" will become "You are my people." In response to this great love we will say, "You are my Husband; you are my God" (see Hos. 2:23). Consider the Lord's words of love and take them to heart:

> How can I give you up, O Ephraim?
> How can I hand you over, O Israel? . . .
> My heart recoils within me;
> my compassion grows warm and tender. (Hos. 11:8)

Dear brother, dear sister, you are not alone. You are not a deserted divorcée; that is not your identity. No matter what has happened to you in your life; no matter how you've sinned or been sinned against, your identity is that of a beloved, pure bride. The Lord has not given up on you or turned away in cold disdain. He is not waiting to visit his wrath upon you. No, his compassion toward us is warm and tender. Over and over he woos us, reaching out hands of love to embrace us in full marital bliss. No matter what you've suffered at the hands of others, this is a husband you can trust. You can turn toward him; you can trust him to love and welcome you. He will not desert you. You can allow yourself to enjoy his embrace without fear that he will take advantage of you, rape you, hurt you, or shame you into submitting to his misuse of you. We are his people, and his disposition toward us is a disposition of mercy, gentleness, and compassion, not anger, hatred, or desertion.

So many times I find myself trying to keep a safe distance from the Lord. I know that he loves me, but I'm not sure that what he has for me is good. So I hide and busy myself with many amusements. But this hiding carries with it a great impoverishment of heart; I long to be loved and welcomed, and I try to answer that longing in any of a thousand ways. I think I'm keeping myself from being hurt, that I don't need to be open to him and so vulnerable all the time, and it is in that very distrust that I wound myself again and again. And still he stands with loving arms speaking tenderly to me, "How can I give you up, O Elyse? How can I hand you over, O _____ [insert your name here]? My heart recoils within me; my compassion grows warm and tender." His love is unceasing. He is a faithful husband.

## CALLED BY HIS NAME

In ancient times, people did not have last names as we do today. For instance, at my birth, I would have been known simply as "Elyse, Jerome's daughter." Now that I am a married woman, I would be called, "Elyse, Phil's wife." My children would be known as "Phil's sons" or "Phil's daughter." In fact, my last name, Fitzpatrick, actually means "son of Patrick," so we can assume that at some time in my husband's lineage, there was a man whose name was Patrick who had a son. I'm "Elyse, Phil's wife, son of Patrick."

Until recent times, everyone bore the name of his or her family of origin. The tradition of brides taking their husband's last name is still carried on in America today although it is fading away, with some women keeping their last name or hyphenating it with their husband's. These days we're more interested in identifying ourselves as individuals rather than being part of a family group—an inclination that impoverishes us and heightens our innate sense of isolation.

Because we are Jesus's bride, he has given us his name. You'll remember that the name "Jesus" was first given to him by an angel—it was the name chosen by his Father for the incarnate Son. In ancient times, names actually had meaning, and Jesus's name means "God saves." In naming his Son "Jesus," God was foretelling and describing his son's mission. Jesus had come to "seek and save the lost" (Luke 19:10). From the moment he left heaven and became the Word made flesh until he breathed his last on the cross, Jesus's one mission was to fulfill his name, save his bride, and then bestow upon her his name: "God saves, and God has saved me." In addition to it being an appropriate name for him, it's also an appropriate name for us, too. Who am I? I am Elyse, the one God has saved, the bride of Jesus. Considering our name, our identity, is more than an insignificant diversion; it has been God's purpose from the beginning to have a people called by his name from among all the peoples on the earth, Jew and Gentile alike:

> For I am the LORD your God,
>     the Holy One of Israel, your Savior. . . .
> Because you are precious in my eyes,
>     and honored, and I love you. . . .
> Fear not, for I am with you. . . .
> I will . . . bring my sons from afar
>     and my daughters from the end of the earth,

> everyone who is *called by my name*,
>> whom I created for my glory,
>> whom I formed and made. (Isa. 43:3–7)

And to all peoples he has said,

> I was ready to be sought by those who did not ask for me;
>> I was ready to be found by those who did not seek me.
> I said, "Here I am, here I am,"
>> to a nation that was *not called by my name*. (Isa. 65:1)

And, in response to God's placing his name on the Gentiles in Cornelius's house, James said,

> Simeon has related how God first visited the Gentiles, to take from them a people *for his name*. . . . "And all the Gentiles who are *called by my name*, says the Lord . . ." (Acts 15:14–18)

The naming of Jesus was not arbitrary or insignificant. His name represented his identity and mission, his character. He was sent to be the savior of his people. Our taking of his name in marriage is not arbitrary or insignificant either. We are the bride, his saved ones, and this identification with him will carry on into eternity, for we read that in heaven we will see his face, and his name will be inscribed on our foreheads (Rev. 22:4).

## HIS GOOD NAME

Before Phil and I were married, no one would have said that I had a "good name." Of course, I had become a Christian a couple of years before, but my reputation was not that I came from a fine, upstanding family. I was, rather, a girl from the other side of the tracks and definitely not someone you would want your son to marry. I was that desolate divorcée we discussed earlier. Because of that, one of the factors that drew me to Phil was his family: the Fitzpatricks. They were a strong, godly family with missionaries, pastors, musicians, and evangelists in every branch of their family tree. Yes, I loved (and still do love) Phil personally, but I also loved and wanted the good name of his family. I thought that his name would give me a respectable identity, something I had never had, and something that I longed for. Proverbs says that "a good name is to be chosen rather than great riches" (Prov. 22:1), so I chose Phil and Phil's name. I am Elyse *Fitzpatrick*, respectable woman who married into a respectable family.

In the same way, in giving his good name to us, Jesus has given us his good reputation. Yes, the Fitzpatrick family has a good name, but it's nothing in comparison to the reputation we've been given in receiving Jesus's name. His name is not only "God saves" but is also "the LORD is our righteousness" (Jer. 23:6). "And because of [God] you are in Christ Jesus, who became to us . . . righteousness" (1 Cor. 1:30).

Through marriage Jesus Christ bestows upon us his righteous reputation, but this new name we've been given is more than a superficial reputation pasted over a dirty face, or a diamond ring forced onto a filthy finger. It's an actual change in identity. We have his reputation. We have a reputation that is as if we had his character, and it is that character that is being worked in us. The bestowal of his name upon us actually resurrects us and brings us from death to life. He transfers us from the kingdom of darkness to the kingdom of Christ. We are citizens of a new country. We are truly alive. We are free and no longer enslaved to sin or the law. We are not the people we once were. By faith in his work and in the giving of his name, this transformation reaches to the inmost part of our soul, changes our desires, and frees us from the tyranny of self-righteousness and her twin daughters: self-approval and criticism of others. This glorious transformation has a name: *justification.*

> But you were washed, . . . you were justified in the name of the Lord Jesus Christ and by the Spirit of our God. (1 Cor. 6:11)

## JUSTIFICATION

And now, and at last, we come to the most splendid blessing of our union with Christ, our *justification*. Justification is a term that means that by his grace God has done two wonderful things for us through the life, death, and resurrection of Jesus our husband.

First, by his death in our place, he has forgiven all our sins. The report that represented our entire life—every thought, word and deed; every time we've slighted someone or have been downright mean; every wicked thought; every evil deed; all our sins, large and small, from birth to death—has already been laid upon our Savior-husband's dear back. And then he was punished in our place so that his reputation of never having sinned could be transferred to us—all because he loves you and me. We are forgiven!

Justification means "Just as if I never sinned," and that's exactly how God the Father looks at us. When he sees us, he is happy that we are betrothed to his Son, for he has cast all our sin out of his sight so it's as if we had never sinned. I am, all who believe are, perfect in his sight. That's almost too good to be true, isn't it? We're *that* forgiven? Our reputation is *that* clean? "Behold, the Lamb of God, who takes away the sin of the world!" (John 1:29) Atonement for your sin has already been made. God no longer sees it; he no longer holds it against you. Jesus has done this! "In him we have redemption through his blood, the forgiveness of our trespasses" (Eph. 1:7).

> And you, who were dead in your trespasses and the uncircumcision of your flesh, God made alive together with him, having forgiven us all our trespasses, by canceling the record of debt that stood against us with its legal demands. This he set aside, nailing it to the cross. (Col. 2:13–14)

> Blessed are those whose lawless deeds are forgiven, and whose sins are covered; blessed is the man against whom the Lord will not count his sin. (Rom. 4:7–8)

God has forgiven *all* our sins. He has cancelled out *all* our debt. *All* our lawless deeds are forgiven, now and forever. Our sins are covered. The Lord will not count our sins against us. He has cast our sins behind his back and thrown them into the depths of the sea.

> In love you have delivered my life
>> from the pit of destruction,
> for you have cast all my sins
>> behind your back. (Isa. 38:17)

> He will again have compassion on us;
>> he will tread our iniquities underfoot.
> You will cast all our sins
>> into the depths of the sea. (Mic. 7:19)

Not only has God forgiven all our sins and erased the record of all our wrongdoing so that he no longer sees it, but also he has added to that clean record a list of all of the good works Jesus did as he lived for about thirty-three-and-a-half years, perfectly fulfilling all the law's demands in our place. In other words, just as the first part of our definition is, "Just as if I had never sinned," this second part is, "Just as if I had always obeyed." Think of that. Not only are you forgiven; you've also been blessed with a reputation and record that proclaims you've always done everything you were supposed to do!

Like our Savior, we now possess more than mere innocence. We possess a righteousness that was earned in the crucible of horrendous temptation and suffering. We're in a better position than Adam or Eve before they fell in the garden. They were innocent, but they were on probation, on trial. We, on the other hand, have persevered victoriously through our time of probation; we are not merely innocent, hoping to pass the test someday and hold on till the end. We have already passed it and are forever secured in our righteousness. How can this be? It is because of the righteousness of our Savior-husband, who has given us his name, his record, and his reputation.

> Therefore, as one trespass led to condemnation for all men, so one act of righteousness leads to justification and life for all men. For as by the one man's disobedience the many were made sinners, so by the one man's obedience the many will be made righteous. (Rom. 5:18–19)

This imputation of righteousness is so freeing that it's almost impossible to describe. What would your life look like if you knew beyond a shadow of a doubt that you were loved and that there was nothing you could do to spoil that reality? Glorious truth! We are completely loved, completely welcomed, completely forgiven—no matter what. "For our sake he made him to be sin who knew no sin, so that in him we might become the righteousness of God" (2 Cor. 5:21). We have the righteousness of God; the "righteous requirement of the law" has been fulfilled in us (Rom. 8:4). Right now you have the righteousness of God, because in God's sight and by justification you have fulfilled every requirement he has set. You don't have anything left to prove and nothing left to lose; everything has been accomplished for the bride he loves. Think of it:

> Justification is a judicial act of God, in which He declares, on the basis of the righteousness of Jesus Christ, that all the claims of the law are satisfied with respect to the sinner.[5]

All the claims of the law are satisfied with respect to you if you believe. That is the gospel message. It is believing that Christ has done it all and that his Father loves us enough to give to us the name of his Son—that righteous name above all names, that name that brings with it the character and reputation of the man Christ Jesus.

> In this transaction God appears, not as an absolute Sovereign who simply sets the law aside, but as a righteous Judge, who

acknowledges the infinite merits of Christ as a sufficient basis for justification, and as a gracious Father, who freely forgives and accepts the sinner.[6]

## UNION WITH CHRIST

How are we to think of ourselves? How do we see ourselves now that we have become new people? This objective act of God, an action whereby he declares that we are both forgiven and righteous, does not infuse us with new moral fiber; it is an objective declaration in the courtroom of God whereby he declares that we are not guilty but are justified sinners, and that even though we continue to sin, we are still counted righteous. But this imputed righteousness does affect and transform us, even as we embrace it by faith, and it passes into our consciousness, and we begin to understand what Christ has done. Justification means that we have the same reputation that he has, and that objective truth needs to seep down into our souls. Yes, we are still inwardly unrighteous, but outwardly we have his name.

We are the chosen ones. He has betrothed us to himself, and we've been given immeasurable riches in the dower he has provided for us. He has chosen to love us and to change our name so that we who were known as "No Mercy" and "Not My People" are now free to call him "My Husband."

## FOUND IN HIM

1) How does thinking about yourself as chosen, betrothed, beloved, and named transform you? Which one of those four words speaks most deeply to you? Why?

2) Being "kept" in his name guarantees both provision and protection. In the Old Testament the name of the Lord is pictured as a strong tower (Ps. 61:3; Prov. 18:10). Can you think of any other metaphors for his name?

3) When Christians are said to be "justified in the name" (1 Cor. 6:11), the implication is that the unchangeable nature of Jesus is the ground of our secure possession of all the blessings he has earned. Respond.

4) When speaking of his role as "friend of the bridegroom," John the Baptist said, "The one who has the bride is the bridegroom" (John 3:29). What does the reality of Jesus having you for his bride mean? What does it mean to you particularly?

5) Summarize in four or five sentences what you've learned in this chapter.

# 10

# You Are Forgiven, You Are Righteous, You Are Loved

*But people are counted as righteous, not because of their work,*
*but because of their faith in God who forgives sinners.*

ROMANS 4:5 NLT

Throughout this book I have brought you only one message: Christ's work on your behalf. Beginning with the incarnation, his union with our humanity, to our marriage and union with his person, I have purposely beaten only one drum: *Jesus Christ has already done it all.* He took on human flesh so that he could be our perfect representative. He was tempted in every way that we are, and yet he conquered every temptation perfectly in our place.

His incarnation meant that he was furnished with a human body—a mortal body meant to perish in our place. His daily temptations extended all the way from Bethlehem to the cross, where he was tempted to love himself and his standing before his Father more than he loved us, and yet he persevered so that he could cry out, "It is finished" (John 19:30).

From the councils of eternity past onward through Bethlehem, Nazareth, Jerusalem, Golgotha, and even to Bethany, where he ascended back into heaven, there is just one story, only one subject of all the verbs: Jesus Christ. He is the actor; we are the acted upon. He is the Son, the Savior, the Mediator, the Redeemer, the Groom, the Hero, and the King. And—astounding truth sweeter than all truths—we are his! We are the saved, his brothers and sisters, his redeemed, his bride, citizens of his marvelous kingdom—and will be so forever. He has done all this for us so that we might be one with him, united to him forever and found in his great love and grace. Glorious soul-satisfying, life-transforming news!

As you read the preceding chapters, were you waiting for me to make you the subject of the verbs? Were you waiting me for to tell you what you should do, what five things you need to do to get your "godliness act" together? Well, this is the chapter where we're going to talk about that, but it may not be in the way you expect, because even in this chapter Jesus is going to remain the subject of all the verbs.

## HE HAS SANCTIFIED US

Let's revisit Ephesians 5 to discover what Jesus has done for us, his bride. You'll remember that this passage begins with a command to husbands to love their wives, and then goes on to talk about Christ's work for his bride:

> Husbands, love your wives, as Christ loved the church and gave himself up for her, that he might sanctify her, having cleansed her by the washing of water with the word, so that he might present the church to himself in splendor, without spot or wrinkle or any such thing, that she might be holy and without blemish. (Eph. 5:25–27)

When Paul wrote that the church Christ has given to himself is without "spot," he means that he has removed every stain of sin. Though our sins were "like scarlet," he has made them "white as snow" (Isa. 1:18). He removes every wrinkle, every evidence that we've lived too long in this sin-cursed world and are too set in our ways to ever be young again. All of sin's effects on our souls, all that haggard, worn, and dying loss of hope and joy are removed, and the "skin" of our soul is fresh and young again. Our youth "is renewed like the eagle's" because he has satisfied us with good in having forgiven, healed, redeemed, and crowned us with steadfast love and mercy (Ps. 103:5). When he sees us, we are without blemish; in his eyes we are morally blameless and without fault. We are innocent once again. When on the cross he said, "It is finished," he saw his bride as he had made her: splendid and glorious. He's already done everything that needed to be done. We are the forgiven, the justified, the beloved.

Jesus loved us and gave himself up for us. He did this not only at the end of his life, on the cross, but has been doing it since eternity past when he agreed to come to us and transform us into a church worthy to be his bride. In giving himself up for us, he has sanctified us; that is, by the power of his work and the indwelling of the Spirit he has sent to indwell us, he has set us apart for himself, has declared that we are already holy, and is transforming our nature to be more and more like his. This process of becoming more and more what we already are is called "sanctification." Sanctification begins with his cleansing of us by the word of the gospel. When we hear his declaration, "Your sins are forgiven! You are righteous! We are one!" the Holy Spirit gives us faith to believe that we are what he says we are, and it is through this belief that our character is transformed. So, then, if all that is true, if we are forgiven, righteous, and one with him, how should that change the way we live our lives?

## WHEN CHANGE IS THE PRIMARY MESSAGE

For many people the entire point of Christianity is found here in the topic of *change*. No matter how one might define that word, many of us are primarily interested in how to get better, to be better, and to do more. Rather than spending most of our time reflecting on the incarnation and our union with Christ, the majority of messages and books in the Christian marketplace are about what we're supposed to be doing. The deep and life-transforming message of the incarnation and our union with Jesus is trampled under the stampede of believers trying to find the secret to being a better you.

## HOW JESUS'S WORK TRANSFORMS US

I have purposely avoided talking to you about your obligation to obey, because I wanted to focus your attention tightly on the only aspect of your faith that actually has the power to transform you: the initiating, prior love of God for you in Jesus Christ. In 1 John the beloved disciple wrote, "We love *because* he first loved us" (1 John 4:19). So, then, it follows that if the entire law is summed up by the command to love God and neighbor, and if love comes *only* from the knowledge that he has loved us first, then the avenue to obedience begins by remembering over and over again his love for us in Christ.

Galatians is Paul's great treatise on justification that is by faith rather than by obedience to the law. But even so, in Galatians 5 Paul admonishes the Galatians (and us) to check the freedom we've been given in Christ and not use it as an opportunity to sin or to demand that others serve us or give us what we want. Instead of demanding our own way, as we realize more fully the love freely given to us, we are free to lovingly serve others. We are freed from the law as a way to merit God's love and welcome. Jesus has already given that to us. But we are not free from seeking to fulfill the law of love as an expression of our love for what he's already done. Paul puts this kind of neighbor-serving love in this way: "the whole law is fulfilled in one word: 'You shall love your neighbor as yourself'" (v. 14). Paul believed the message of justification by faith alone, and he knew that this message is the *only* one that will transform us from demanding slaves into loving sons and daughters.

We are justified by faith *alone*. Because of the justification already freely bestowed on us, we are free to serve our neighbors in love. I am free to serve my neighbor because I don't need to demand my rights—I have everything I need in Christ. I am free to serve my neighbor because I don't need to demand to be loved—I have already been fully loved in Christ. I am free to serve my neighbor because I don't need to be respected—Jesus knows exactly who I am, and yet he has given me the position of his queen. I don't need your success or love or approbation or support to make me into a person of worth. My identity is that, right now, I am more loved than I could ever dream. Justification by grace through faith frees me to take my eyes off how I'm doing (and how you're doing) and look to Jesus, who will place neighbors before me who need to be loved today.

I haven't talked about what you need to do in response to God's love before now, because the truths I've spoken to you are the very message that has the power to change you, to make you love God and others, and to free you from your incessant desire to have God and others serve you. It is the message of the first nine chapters of this book that we need to hear over and over and over again and never let slip away from our hearts.

My assumption is that *if all the work he has done and all the love he has shown to you doesn't move your heart to want to respond in love for him, then my telling you to love and obey him won't move you to obedience, either.*

Sure, I could make for you a long checklist of things to do to love God and others, but what would that accomplish? You already know the list: you are to love God with your whole heart, soul, mind, and strength and your neighbor as yourself. Of course, sometimes we don't know what loving God and our neighbor looks like or how we might accomplish that, so lists and accountability are good; but lists and accountability will *never* motivate you to love. We can learn what loving obedience looks like if we want to do it, but only the gospel will actually implant love and a desire to obey in your heart.

I'm sure that for some of you this might seem like a strange concept, so what I want to do now is help you connect the dots between the work Christ has already done and the way in which this work will eventually change your responses to temptation. But I want us to be very careful here. I am not shifting the focus now from Jesus onto us. I simply want to go further into what he's done, making it more personal for you, so that you can know and speak the truth to yourself when you're tempted to forget or think that the message of the incarnation and union are insignificant.

## WE ALL WANT TO BE RIGHTEOUS, OR AT LEAST HAVE EVERYONE ELSE THINK WE ARE (OR PLAY LIKE WE DON'T CARE IF WE ARE)

Let's visit Galatians again and look at the passage that closely follows the command to lovingly serve others that we've been discussing. In Galatians 5:19–21 Paul lists what he calls the "works of the flesh":

> Sexual immorality, impurity, sensuality, idolatry, sorcery, enmity, strife, jealousy, fits of anger, rivalries, dissensions, divisions, envy, drunkenness, orgies, and things like these. I warn you, as I warned you before, that those who do such things will not inherit the kingdom of God.

These selfish thoughts, words, and deeds are merely what comes of thinking that we are responsible to make ourselves right in our own eyes and in the eyes of others.

### Sexual Immorality

For instance, sexual immorality, impurity, and sensuality all flow out of a desire to feel good about yourself, your sexual prowess, your ability to attract others, to be desirable; it is the belief that pleasure and being desired by another will justify your existence and make you okay with yourself.

Some people throw themselves headlong into a destructively promiscuous lifestyle because they've given up hope that they'll ever get what they desire most of all: real love and true righteousness. Before I came to Christ, I used my sexuality in this way. I was looking for love, for someone to tell me that I was okay, and I thought I could find it in relationships with men.

I know that men too struggle with pornography and illicit relationships, at least in part because they long to be desired and want to prove that they are real men who really are okay. Of course, the pleasure of illicit sex is a strong temptation, but even that pleasure is fleeting and produces terrible feelings of guilt that only the gospel can ultimately assuage. Can you see how the gospel provides the true answer to sexual immorality?

Men, you are forgiven and loved. The pleasure you feel when you look at pornography, the way you are willing for other men to enslave and use your sisters for your pleasure, has been forgiven. Jesus paid the price for that. Unless you believe that he is looking at you in love right now, the guilt you feel will impel you to click again. He has removed every stain of sin. He loves you now and is praying for you. You don't need to pursue sexual "freedom" (which is actually slavery) because you've already been given true freedom in Christ. You are no longer enslaved to the law's demands, demands that you can never meet. In addition, you are no longer enslaved to sin with no hope of change. Jesus has made you his own and given you the "freedom of the glory of the children of God" (Rom. 8:21). You are indwelt by the Holy Spirit, who is working in you even now.

Women, you are forgiven and loved. You have been desired by a man—not by some man who wants to use you up and throw you away but by a righteous husband who has given up everything for your benefit and stands praying for you now. No matter whether you are single or married, your earthly marital status is not your primary identity. Your primary identity is glorious, splendid bride without spot, wrinkle, or blemish. You don't need to live your life in constant pursuit of the perfect body or face or hair so that you can attract a man and prove to be desirable. Jesus sees you as you are and has forgiven you. No matter what you've done. No matter if you've plunged into a lesbian relationship or had seven abortions. You're loved and forgiven *now*. You're more than what you once were; your shameful identity is gone. You're more than a little girl who has been abused or a prostitute who has abused herself and sold herself for one more high. You're Christ's bride. He's done everything to make you his. You are forgiven. You are righteous.

## IDOLATRY AND SORCERY

Idolatry and sorcery are unlawful means of getting some deity to give you what you want, whether that's a good crop (so that you can approve of yourself and brag about your wealth) or a glimpse of the future (so that you can have power over others or plan for future events, or so that you'll look good and not be left flat-footed, looking like a fool).

You can identify your idolatry or what might be called "functional idols" by looking at the desires that drive you to sin. What is it that you want so much you're willing to sin to get it? What is it that you think you have been cheated out of? Where do you think true happiness comes from? Whatever those things are, and we all struggle with them, those are your idols.[1] Idolatry is crushed beneath true worship. When you turn your eyes away from all that you think you need and look instead at the one who lived and died and rose again and is waiting for you, loving worship will be a natural response. Think of it: Jesus has already suffered for all your idolatries, for every time you worshiped something or someone other than him. You are forgiven. You are righteous. You are loved. You don't need what those other gods are promising you; you already have everything in him.

My guess is that most Christians don't play with Ouija boards or Magic 8 Balls or cast spells using voodoo dolls. Sorcery? Not us! But I wonder how many gamble or play the lottery. There is absolutely no way for you to do these things without believing in some sort of superstition. Whenever you feel that it's your *lucky day*, or that this is a *lucky machine*, repent and believe the gospel.

Jesus Christ, the Ancient of Days (Dan. 7:9) stands over every day and has bestowed upon you every benefit you need.

Here's the good news: you don't need anything more than you already have. You don't need great wealth or status or cars or "luck" (a truly meaningless word). You are forgiven. You are justified. You are blessed. You are loved. You don't need to have bigger houses or assure yourself of your worth because you know how to play the ponies or beat the system or because some person finally approves of you. Jesus has paid it all, given it all, and loved you immeasurably.

## RELATIONAL CONFLICTS

Enmity, strife, jealousy, fits of anger, rivalries, dissensions, divisions, and envy are all evidences of what James calls "the lusts" or "desires" that war within your heart and cause fights and quarrels (see James 4:1–2). Where do these destructive desires come from? Pride. In every one of these conflicts, you should see God's hand opposing the proud. The conflicts themselves are meant to tell you something; they're meant to tell you that you are still fighting for your piece of the pie, you're still warring to get your place in the sun, or at least a little bit of respect. Every time you sin against your neighbor, the guilt you feel for doing so will create a greater hatred for him. Guilt at failing to love your neighbor never creates love for your neighbor. It only creates more bad feelings and more of a desire to justify yourself by focusing on all the ways he's hurt you.

But the truths of the gospel change that. The fact that you are loved and forgiven means that you can love and forgive others—even those who have been unloving and unforgiving to you—because you need no other love than the love you've been given. Sure, good friends and close families are a wonderful gift, but they're not a necessity. The truth about what Jesus has already done for you should speak to your heart and enable you to humble yourself and remember the forgiveness and righteousness that comes from the mighty warrior Jesus Christ. He has shouldered all of God's fury in his own body and put aside all the conflict, reconciling you to God and overcoming all the conflict that you had initiated between yourself and his Father.

Every time you yell at a driver who cuts you off, what you are saying in essence is that you are filled with pride and crave his respect. God opposes you in this, so you experience the discomfort of conflict.

Every time you look at something someone else has and self-ishly want it for yourself, you're demonstrating that you believe that that thing (whatever it is) will bring you happiness and a sense that you're as good as that other guy after all. God is opposing you in your envy and making you uncomfortable so that you will turn to him in humble gratitude.

Every time you gossip about a coworker who dissed you at the water cooler, it's because you still think that in order to be okay, you need to be respected. The reason you think you need to be respected is that you're not remembering that you've already been justified; you already have the best reputation possible because of what Christ has done. When you remember this truth, you will also know that being respected by another driver, friend, coworker, or spouse is nothing and paltry in comparison. You don't need to be respected; you are justified. Jesus has earned for you what you could never earn by all your work to be respected: a perfect reputation as his beautiful bride.

You can put your weapons of war down, whether those weapons are your cutting and vicious words, your pouting and coldness, your gossip or slander, or any combination of any of the ways you create conflict in this world and in your family by your pride and pursuit of something more. You don't need to fight anymore to be right. The fight has been won. You are forgiven. You are righteous. Who cares if you get dissed? Who cares if you lose at office politics? You've won the love of your God through no effort of your own.

If anyone would come after me, let him deny himself and take up his cross daily and follow me. For whoever would save his life will lose it, but whoever loses his life for my sake will save it. For what does it profit a man if he gains the whole world and loses or forfeits himself? (Luke 9:23-25)

## LIFE AS THE ENDLESS (AND EMPTY) PARTY

Drunkenness and orgies are simply a habitually inflated desire to drown your sense of guilt, worthlessness, shame, and emptiness at a party. The thought is that if there is just enough booze and sex, if the music is loud enough, if your behavior is outrageous enough, if you could just swear enough or fornicate enough, you might, at least for one moment of pleasure, be able to drown out your conscience's accusatory voice and feel that you're okay after all. Of course, the sad reality is that no matter how many women (or men) you bed, no matter how many fifths of gin you down and then puke up on the bathroom floor, you'll never feel justified until you find your justification in the work of another.

You can turn the music down. You can begin to love others and lay down your life because you are loved. You don't need to wake up on the morning after and hope you didn't kill anyone on your way home or contract a disease this time. You can rest, finally rest. Sweet, pure rest is yours through the work that Jesus has already done.

> Come to me, all who labor and are heavy laden, and I will give you rest. Take my yoke upon you, and learn from me, for I am gentle and lowly in heart, and you will find rest for your souls. For my yoke is easy, and my burden is light. (Matt. 11:28–30)

Do you like parties? I do. Good parties are a great good, and the best party ever is still to come. It's called the "marriage supper of the Lamb," and it will be the party of the ages (Rev. 19:9). And you are the blessed who is invited! As a matter of fact, you're the bride. It's your party, the party heaven is throwing because the work of the Son and the work of his bride is finished. This will be one party at which you won't be ashamed of yourself, where you won't wonder if this is finally the last straw; the one party at which everyone will love each other. This is the party at which you can look at yourself and know that you've been loved. Jesus has already forgiven you for all your drunkenness and orgies and never-ending labor to feel good and have some fun. He saw all that and bore his Father's wrath for it on the cross. Flee to him. He's worth it. You are forgiven. You are loved.

Can you see how every one of these works of the flesh are directly tied to a neglect of the truths of what God has done for you in Christ? To live habitually in them is a sign that you haven't yet believed the freeing good news of Jesus's work on your behalf. In saying that, I'm not saying that Christians don't struggle, and at times terribly, with these things. I do think, though, that Paul's point is that that those who make a habitual practice of doing them, who live in them as a pattern of life, will not inherit the kingdom of God. If you truly believe that God has loved you, then you *will*, sometimes more but at other times barely at all, love him and your neighbor in response, and you will not live totally and habitually as though he didn't love you at all.

## THESE WORKS ARE THE RESULTS OF YOUR WORKS

These "works" of the flesh are the result of your working instead of believing. They flow out of your belief that you need to get yourself something more than what Christ has already provided, that you need to work to attain righteousness or "okay-ness" or pleasure on your own. Whenever you think you need something that Christ hasn't provided through his incarnation and work for you, then you are working to supply your own righteousness, and this work will always, *always*, eventuate in these sins (and others like them). When the focus of your life is on yourself and your progress (or lack thereof), you will always struggle with these works of the flesh and with the guilt that underlies every failure. And guilt *never* motivates loving obedience. It may make you try to stop sinning in some way so that you'll feel better about yourself, but it will never produce obedience that is God honoring. That's because God-honoring obedience *must* be motivated by "faith working through love" (Gal. 5:6), not the desire to approve of yourself.

Just think for a moment about the sins you struggle with, whatever they may be. I guarantee that at their root is the desire to approve of yourself, to have others approve of you, or to anesthetize your soul to the reality of your failure to be okay. It is because of this inevitable result of your self-righteous work that I have purposely avoided telling you to get to work. Unless your heart and soul are deeply rooted in the forgiveness and righteousness obtained for you by Jesus Christ, you will continue to struggle to love, to serve, to put off sinful habits, and to put on grateful obedience. Of course, you'll continue to struggle with sin while you live here, but the struggle will take a on a different cast; it will be a struggle with confident hope at the end.

## BEARING MUCH FRUIT

The key to an obedient life lies not in doing something more, not in making New Year's resolutions or longer lists, but rather in believing the truth more deeply. Jerry Bridges writes,

> We are to count on or believe the fact that we actually did die to the guilt and consequent dominion of sin. . . . We are to believe we truly have been set free. Not only are we to believe we have died to sin; we are also to believe we are alive unto God, united to the risen Christ, and partakers of his divine nature. It is the belief of this truth that will give us the courage not to let sin reign in our mortal bodies. And it is through reliance upon this truth that we will experience the power of His Spirit, who dwells within us to enable us to resist the motions of sin so that it is not able to reign in us.[2]

This striving to believe, striving to remember and rest (Heb. 4:11) in all he has done for us, is what it means to "abide" in Jesus as the vine, and it's the hardest work you will ever do.

I am the true vine, and my Father is the vinedresser. Every branch in me that does not bear fruit he takes away, and every branch that does bear fruit he prunes, that it may bear more fruit. Already you are clean because of the word that I have spoken to you. Abide in me, and I in you. . . . As the branch cannot bear fruit by itself, unless it abides in the vine, neither can you, unless you abide in me. I am the vine; you are the branches. Whoever abides in me and I in him, he it is that bears much fruit, for apart from me you can do nothing. . . . As the Father has loved me, so have I loved you. Abide in my love. (John 15:1–5, 9)

Jesus and all he has done for us is the vine. The Father watches over the branches of the vine, prunes them and making them fruitful by feeding them with the word that Jesus has spoken to us through the gospel message. We are forgiven. We are righteous. We are loved.

What is our responsibility? What will cause fruit to grow from our lives? We are to abide in him and recognize that he abides in us. These words should remind you of *union* language. Remember how we are in him and he is in us? The hard work of abiding doesn't mean that we work strenuously to hang on but rather that we rest and remember what he has done, and remain or keep our hearts and minds there. Do you want to be fruitful in your life? Your primary need is not a list of things to do. You need a list of what he's done. We remain or abide in our forgiveness. We remain or abide in imputed righteousness. We remain or abide in his love for us. We don't try to work up our own forgiveness or righteousness or to merit his love, and whenever we find ourselves thirsting after pleasure or are angry, worried, despairing or apathetic, we'll know that's just what we've been doing.

Then, as we abide in him, remembering and resting on the work he has done and the life he is providing, we *will* bear much fruit. How does this happen? By our working hard to prove we're really okay after all? No, of course not. It is by resting or abiding in his love. "As the Father has loved me, so have I loved you.

Abide in my love." Abiding means that we remember who he is, who we are, and what he's done for us. It is in that freedom from guilt, freedom from trying to work up God's favor, freedom from trying to make ourselves presentable or respectable that we find fruit growing in our lives in surprising and delightful ways.

## BEHOLD THE MAN

I pray that the Holy Spirit has so worked in your heart that you are beginning to know how loved, how forgiven, how justified, how righteous, and how free you are because of what he's done. I pray that you are allowing yourself to suspend your unbelief, your works-righteousness, and your worries and fears, and that you're beginning to rest in his loving arms.

It is my belief that the more you rest in him, the more you get your eyes off yourself, your desires, your sins, and your progress, the more frequently you'll be surprised by the sweet fruit growing in your heart. Then it will be on some typical day that you'll look at the way in which you have responded to someone and say,

*Wow. That's different. I'm not as anxious or angry or worried or fearful or demanding as I used to be. I feel at peace even in the midst of this chaos.*

And then you'll be grateful—not that you've completed your list but that he completed his for you. I'm not saying that thinking about the incarnation and our union with Christ is magic. What I am saying is that the more you focus on how loved you are and how everything you need has already been given to you, the more peace, rest, and love you'll experience. As his truth comforts and assures you, you'll find that you don't have to fight or worry or envy anymore. You can rest, and in that rest you will find a sweetness growing in your soul that will delight and nourish those around you. And in every way you fail, when you fall back into patterns of unbelief and striving, you'll find the grace to wholeheartedly and transparently repent, knowing that your sin problem has already been taken care of and that you are forgiven.

## IT REALLY HAS ALWAYS BEEN ALL ABOUT HIM

Now that our time together is drawing to a close, let me leave you with some encouragements.

First, let me remind you that Jesus Christ has done it all. He took human flesh to himself and lived perfectly in your place. He has done everything that needed to be done to bring you in from your exile, isolation, and death. He did this by condescending to take human flesh to himself so that he might be the perfect representative you needed; he is your brother, your husband. He was exiled and isolated for you. He died in your place, paying the price demanded by his holy Father.

He has done everything necessary to be united to you. He has made you a beautiful bride and has already gone into heaven to prepare a beautiful home for you. Right now he is waiting for you, watching over you, providing for and protecting you. Like a good husband, he is praying for you on your journey.

If you believe these truths, nothing will ever separate you from his love for you. You can't mess this up. You didn't earn it, so you can't forfeit it. It is all his gift of love. He is yours. You are his. Forever.

> Celebrate Immanuel's Name, the Prince of life and peace.
> God with us, our lips proclaim, our faithful hearts confess.
> God is in our flesh revealed; Heav'n and earth in Jesus join.
> Mortal with Immortal filled, and human with Divine.
>
> Fullness of the Deity in Jesus' body dwells,
> Dwells in all His saints and me when God His Son reveals.
> Father, manifest Thy Son; breathe the true incarnate Word.
> In our inmost souls make known the presence of the Lord.
>
> Let the Spirit of our Head through every member flow;
> By our Lord inhabited, we then Immanuel know.
> Then He doth His Name express; God in us we truly prove,
> Find with all the life of grace and all the power of love.
>
> —Charles Wesley

## FOUND IN HIM

1) Paul wrote,

> For we are the circumcision, who worship by the Spirit of God
> and glory in Christ Jesus and put no confidence in the flesh—
> though I myself have reason for confidence in the flesh also. If
> anyone else thinks he has reason for confidence in the flesh, I
> have more: circumcised on the eighth day, of the people of Israel,
> of the tribe of Benjamin, a Hebrew of Hebrews; as to the law, a
> Pharisee; as to zeal, a persecutor of the church; as to righteous-
> ness under the law, blameless. But whatever gain I had, I counted
> as loss for the sake of Christ. Indeed, I count everything as loss
> because of the surpassing worth of knowing Christ Jesus my Lord.
> For his sake I have suffered the loss of all things and count them
> as rubbish, in order that I may gain Christ and be found in him,
> not having a righteousness of my own that comes from the law,
> but that which comes through faith in Christ, the righteousness
> from God that depends on faith—that I may know him and the
> power of his resurrection, and may share his sufferings, becom-
> ing like him in his death, that by any means possible I may attain
> the resurrection from the dead. (Phil. 3:3–11)

How did Paul fight his propensity to trust in his own righteousness? What
kind of righteousness did he have? How fruitful was he?

2) As you consider the list of the "works of the flesh" in Galatians 5, which
ones do you struggle with most? How can recognizing your forgiveness
and righteousness in Christ change you?

3) Summarize in four or five sentences what you have learned in this
chapter.

4) Review all the summaries you've already written at the end of each
chapter and summarize them all. What did you learn in this book? What
was most meaningful to you? What will you do to try to remember what
you've learned?

# Appendix 1

# The Creeds

After Jesus's resurrection and ascension, his identity was so hotly debated that it became the topic of the first four church councils and the subject of the creeds that the early church fathers developed. As modern American evangelicalism has become increasingly less committed to the creeds as a way to define what we all must believe to truly bear the name "Christian," real confusion again colors every part of the incarnation story. This confusion has resulted in a multitude of quasi-Christian cults that bear no resemblance to the original belief system that our forefathers died proclaiming. Make no mistake about it: the primary reason that many men and women suffered martyrdom is that they would not stop proclaiming that God had become man in Jesus Christ.

Here's a summary statement about the incarnation that will help us as we unpack this mystery:

> God, in his wisdom, ordained a combination of human and divine influence in the birth of Christ, so that his full humanity would be evident to us from the fact of his ordinary human birth from a human mother, and his full deity would be evident from the fact of his conception in Mary's womb by the powerful work of the Holy Spirit.[1]

Our modern-day confusion is easily seen in a couple of ways. First, we're very comfortable referring to Jesus as "God," which of course he is, without making any distinction between God the Father and God the Son. For instance, while to say, "God died on the cross," is in one sense true, it would be better to be more precise and say, "God the Son [or Jesus] died on the cross." Neither God the Father nor the Trinity died on the cross. That would have been impossible and would have meant the end of all things.

I don't want to be overly finicky, but imprecision in talking about God is really very significant. Many of the objections the uninitiated have about Christianity flow out of our imprecision. And even more of the false religions or cults flow out of imprecision, especially about the nature of Jesus Christ.[2]

On the other hand, many of us also sing songs about Jesus as if he were our boyfriend or cosmic therapist. I don't mean to be overly critical of certain songwriters, but it would be a good idea if those who wrote contemporary songs for the church had some theological training. And while it is true that Jesus is our heavenly bridegroom, we should not sing about him as if he is just our boyfriend. If I could sing a particular song to my boyfriend, it isn't appropriate to sing in church. It is also true that Christ satisfies all of our deepest needs, but his work is so much more than that and certainly was not primarily that. My guess is that we write songs about Jesus boyfriend-therapist because we've lost the understanding that what we primarily need is Jesus savior-justifier. Aside from it being so very theologically imprecise, Jesus boyfriend-therapist becomes trite and boring way too fast.

## A SHORT HISTORY OF THE CREEDS

The Council of Constantinople met to clarify and refute the Christology of Apollinarius, bishop of Laodicea. Apollinarius insisted that Jesus was a heavenly man dissimilar to earthly men. A human is body, soul, and spirit, so the bishop asserted that Jesus was a body, soul, and *Logos* (literally, "Word"), a man not having a human spirit, or mind. Against this doctrine, the council affirmed the full humanity of Christ.

The Council of Ephesus considered the "marriage Christology" of Nestorius, bishop of Constantinople. He held that the union of the human and divine in Jesus was like the marriage of a husband and wife. As a result, the council accused him of teaching that there were two separate persons in Christ.

The Council of Chalcedon was perhaps the most significant church council for Christianity. It met in debate over the teaching of Eutyches, a monk from Constantinople. He denied that Jesus had two natures. This reaction against the Christology of Nestorius prompted the council to express the incarnation of Jesus in terms of one person with two natures—human and divine.

The mystery of the incarnation continues, and the statements of the first four councils of the Christian church preserve that mystery. Jesus, God incarnate, was one person in two natures—fully divine and fully human.

## THE APOSTLES' CREED (ABOUT AD 390)

I believe in God the Father Almighty, Maker of heaven and earth.

And in Jesus Christ, His only Son, our Lord; who was conceived by the Holy Ghost, born of the Virgin Mary; suffered under Pontius Pilate, was crucified, dead, and buried; He descended into hell; the third day He rose again from the dead; He ascended into heaven, and sitteth on the right hand of God the Father Almighty; from thence He shall come to judge the quick and the dead.

I believe in the Holy Ghost; the holy catholic [universal] Church; the communion of saints; the forgiveness of sins; the resurrection of the body; and the life everlasting. Amen.

## THE NICENE CREED (AD 325)

I believe in one God, the Father Almighty, Maker of heaven and earth, and of all things visible and invisible.

And in one Lord Jesus Christ, the only-begotten Son of God, begotten of the Father before all worlds, God of God, Light of Light, very God of very God; begotten, not made, being of one substance with the Father, by whom all things were made; who for us men, and for our salvation, came down from heaven, and was incarnate by the Holy Ghost of the Virgin Mary, and was made man, and was crucified also for us under Pontius Pilate; He suffered and was buried; and the third day He rose again according to the Scriptures; and ascended into heaven, and sitteth on the right hand of the Father; and He shall come again with glory to judge the quick and the dead; whose kingdom shall have no end.

And I believe in the Holy Ghost, the Lord and Giver of life, who proceedeth from the Father and the Son; who with the Father and the Son together is worshiped and glorified; who spake by the prophets. And I believe in one holy catholic [universal] and apostolic church. I acknowledge one Baptism for the remission of sins; and I look for the resurrection of the dead, and the life of the world to come. Amen.

## THE ATHANASIAN CREED
## (FIFTH OR SIXTH CENTURY AD)

Whosoever will be saved, before all things it is necessary that he hold the catholic faith. Which faith except every one do keep whole and undefiled, without doubt he shall perish everlastingly.

And the catholic faith is this: that we worship one God in Trinity, and Trinity in Unity; Neither confounding the Persons, nor dividing the Substance. For there is one Person of the Father, another of the Son, and another of the Holy Ghost. But the Godhead of the Father, of the Son, and of the Holy Ghost is all one: the glory equal, the majesty coeternal. Such as the Father is, such is the Son, and such is the Holy Ghost. The Father uncreated, the Son uncreated, and the Holy Ghost uncreated. The Father incomprehensible, the Son incomprehensible, and the Holy Ghost incomprehensible. The Father eternal, the Son eternal, and the Holy Ghost eternal. And yet they are not three Eternals, but one Eternal. As there are not three Uncreated nor three Incomprehensibles, but one Uncreated and one Incomprehensible. So likewise the Father is almighty, the Son almighty, and the Holy Ghost almighty. And yet they are not three Almighties, but one Almighty. So the Father is God, the Son is God, and the Holy Ghost is God. And yet they are not three Gods, but one God. So likewise the Father is Lord, the Son Lord, and the Holy Ghost Lord. And yet not three Lords, but one Lord. For like as we are compelled by the Christian verity to acknowledge every Person by Himself to be God and Lord, So are we forbidden by the catholic religion to say, There be three Gods, or three Lords.

The Father is made of none: neither created nor begotten. The Son is of the Father alone; not made, nor created, but begotten. The Holy Ghost is of the Father and of the Son: neither made, nor created, nor begotten, but proceeding. So there is one Father, not three Fathers; one Son, not three Sons; one Holy Ghost, not three Holy Ghosts. And in this Trinity none is before or after another; none is greater or less than another; But the whole three Persons are coeternal together, and coequal: so that in all things, as is aforesaid, the Unity in Trinity and the Trinity in Unity is to be worshiped. He, therefore, that will be saved must thus think of the Trinity.

Furthermore, it is necessary to everlasting salvation that he also believe faithfully the incarnation of our Lord Jesus Christ. For the right faith is, that we believe and confess that our Lord Jesus Christ, the Son of God, is God and Man; God of the Substance of the Father, begotten before the worlds; and Man of the substance of His mother, born in the world; Perfect God and perfect Man, of a reasonable soul and human flesh subsisting. Equal to the Father as touching His Godhead, and inferior to the Father as touching His manhood; Who, although He be God and Man, yet He is not two, but one Christ: One, not by conversion of the Godhead into flesh, but by taking the manhood into God; One altogether; not by confusion of Substance, but by unity of Person. For as the reasonable soul and flesh is one man, so God and Man is one Christ; Who suffered for our salvation; descended into hell, rose again the third day from the dead; He ascended into heaven; He sitteth on the right hand of the Father, God Almighty; from thence He shall come to judge the quick and the dead. At whose coming all men shall rise again with their bodies, and shall give an account of their own works. And they that have done good shall go into life everlasting; and they that have done evil, into everlasting fire.

This is the catholic faith; which except a man believe faithfully and firmly, he cannot be saved.

# Appendix 2

# The Best News Ever

I didn't begin to understand the gospel until the summer before my twenty-first birthday. Although I had attended church from time to time in my childhood, I'll admit that it never really transformed me in any significant way. I was frequently taken to Sunday school where I heard stories about Jesus. I knew, without really understanding, the importance of Christmas and Easter. I remember looking at the beautiful stained-glass windows, with their cranberry red and deep cerulean blue, with Jesus knocking on a garden door, and having a vague sense that being religious was good. But I didn't have the foggiest idea about the gospel.

My strongest memories of adolescence contain despair and anger. I was consistently in trouble, and I hated everyone who pointed that out. There were nights when I prayed that I would be good or, more specifically, get out of whatever trouble I was in and do better, only to be disappointed and angered by the failures of the following day.

Upon graduation from high school at seventeen, I got married, had a baby, and became divorced—all before the third decade of my life began. It was during the following months and years that I discovered the anesthetizing effects of drugs, alcohol, and illicit relationships. Although I was known as a girl who liked to party, I was utterly lost and joyless, and I was beginning to know it.

At one point, I can remember telling a friend that I felt like I was fifty years old, which, at that point in my life, was the oldest I could imagine anyone being. I was exhausted and disgusted, so I decided to set about improving myself. I worked a full-time job, took a full course load at a local junior college, and cared for my son. I changed my living arrangements and tried to start over. I didn't know that the Holy Spirit was working in my heart, calling me to the Son. I just knew that something had to change. Don't misunderstand—I was still living a shamefully wicked life; it's just that I felt that I was beginning to wake up to something different.

At this point, Julie entered my life. She was my next-door neighbor, and she was a Christian. She was kind to me, and we became fast friends. She had a quality of life about her that attracted me, and she was always talking to me about her Savior, Jesus. She let me know that she was praying for me and would frequently encourage me to "get saved." Although I'd had that Sunday school training, what she had to say was something completely different from what I'd ever remembered hearing. She told me I needed to be born again.

And so, on a warm night sometime in June of 1971, I knelt down in my tiny apartment and told the Lord that I wanted to be his. At that point, I didn't really understand much about the gospel, but I did understand this: I was desperate, and I desperately believed that the Lord would help me. That prayer on that night changed everything about me. I remember it now, forty-two years later, as if it were yesterday.

I knew I needed to be saved, and I trusted that Christ could save me. One man who came in contact with some of Jesus's followers asked this same question: "What must I do to be saved?" The answer was simple: "Believe in the Lord Jesus, and you will be saved."

Very simply, what do you need to believe in order to be a Christian? You need to know that you need salvation, help, or deliverance. You must not try to reform yourself or decide that you're going to become a moral person so that God will be impressed.

Because he is completely holy, that is, perfectly moral, you have to give up any idea that you can be good enough to meet his standard. This is the good bad news. It's bad news because it tells you that you're in an impossible situation that you cannot change. But it's also good news because it will free you from endless cycles of self-improvement that end in ultimate failure.

You also need to trust that what you're unable to do—live a perfectly holy life—he's done for you. This is the good *good* news. This is the gospel. Basically, the gospel is the story of how God looked down through the corridors of time and set his love on his people. At a specific point in time, he sent his Son into the world to become fully like us. This is the story you hear about at Christmas. This baby grew to be a man, and after thirty years of obscurity he began to show the people who he was. He did this by performing miracles, healing the sick, and raising the dead. He also demonstrated his deity by teaching people what God required of them and continually foretold his coming death and resurrection. And he did one more thing: he claimed to be God.

Because of his claim to be God, the leading religious people, along with the political powers of the day, passed an unjust sentence of death upon him. Although he had never done anything wrong, he was beaten, mocked, and shamefully executed. He died. Even though it looked like he had failed, the truth is that this was God's plan from the very beginning.

His body was taken down from the cross and laid hastily in a rock tomb in a garden. After three days, some of his followers went to go properly care for his remains and discovered that he had risen from the dead. They actually spoke with him, touched him, and ate with him. This is the story that we celebrate at Easter. After another forty days, he was taken back up into heaven, still in his physical form, and his followers were told that he would return to earth in just the same way.

I told you that there were two things you need to know and believe. The first is that you need more significant help than you or any other mere human could ever supply. The second need is to believe that Jesus, the Christ, is the person who will supply that help and that if you come to him, he will not turn his back on you. You don't need to understand much more than that, and if you really believe these truths, your life will be transformed by his love.

Below I've written out some verses from the Bible for you. As you read them, you can talk to God, just as though he were sitting right by you (because his presence is everywhere!) and ask him for help to understand. Remember, your help isn't based on your ability to perfectly understand or anything that you can do. If you trust him, he's promised to help you, and that's all you need to know for now.

All have sinned and fall short of the glory of God. (Rom. 3:23)

The wages of sin is death, but the free gift of God is eternal life in Christ Jesus our Lord. (Rom. 6:23)

For while we were still weak, at the right time Christ died for the ungodly. For one will scarcely die for a righteous person—though perhaps for a good person one would dare even to die—but God shows his love for us in that while we were still sinners, Christ died for us. (Rom. 5:6–8)

For our sake he made him to be sin who knew no sin, so that in him we might become the righteousness of God. (2 Cor. 5:21)

If you confess with your mouth that Jesus is Lord and believe in your heart that God raised him from the dead, you will be saved. For with the heart one believes and is justified, and with the mouth one confesses and is saved. For the Scripture says, "Everyone who believes in him will not be put to shame." . . . The same Lord is Lord of all, bestowing his riches on all who call on him. For "everyone who calls on the name of the Lord will be saved." (Rom. 10:9–13)

Whoever comes to me I will never cast out. (John 6:37)

Therefore, if anyone is in Christ, he is a new creation. The old has passed away; behold, the new has come. (2 Cor. 5:17)

Come to me, all who labor and are heavy laden, and I will give you rest. Take my yoke upon you, and learn from me, for I am gentle and lowly in heart, and you will find rest for your souls. (Matt. 11:28–29)

There is therefore now no condemnation for those who are in Christ Jesus. (Rom. 8:1)

If you'd like to, you might pray a prayer something like this:

Dear God,

I'll admit that I don't understand everything about this, but I do believe these two things: I need help, and you want to help me. I confess that I'm like Elyse and have pretty much ignored you my whole life, except when I was in trouble or just wanted to feel good about myself. I know that I haven't loved you or my neighbor, so it's true that I deserve to be punished and really do need help. But I also believe that you've brought me here, right now, to read this page because you are willing to help me and that if I ask you for help, you won't send me away empty-handed. I'm beginning to understand how you punished your Son in my place and how, because of his sacrifice for me, I can have a relationship with you.

Father, please guide me to a good church and help me understand your word. I give my life to you and ask you to make me yours.

In Jesus's name, amen.

Here are two more thoughts. First, in his kindness, Jesus established his church to encourage and help us understand and live out these two truths. If you know that you need help, and you think Jesus is able to supply that help, or if you're still questioning but want to know more, please search out a good church in your neighborhood and begin to make relationships there. A good church is one that recognizes we cannot save ourselves by our own goodness and that relies wholly on Jesus Christ (and no one else) for this salvation. You can call around and ask these questions, or you can even go on the Internet and get a listing of churches in your area. Usually they will have something called a "statement of faith" on their website, where you can get information about them. Mormons and Jehovah's Witnesses are not Christian churches, and they do not believe in the gospel (though they might tell you that they do), so you don't want to go there. Finding a good church is sometimes quite a process, so don't be discouraged if you don't succeed right away. Keep trying and believing that God will help you.

Second, another factor that will help you grow in this new life of faith is to begin to read what God has said about himself and about us in his Word, the Bible. In the New Testament (the last one-third or so of the Bible), there are four Gospels or narratives about the life of Jesus. I recommend that you start with the first one, Matthew, and then work your way through the other three. I recommend that you purchase a good modern translation, such as the English Standard Version, but you can get any version (though not a paraphrase) that you're comfortable with and begin reading more right away.

The last request that I have of you is that you contact me through my website, http://www.elysefitzpatrick.com, if you've decided while reading this book that you want to follow Jesus. Thank you for taking time to read this little explanation of the most important news you'll ever hear. You can read this book and trust that the Lord will help you understand and become what he wants you to be: a person who's been so loved by him that you're transformed in both your identity and life.

# Appendix 3

# John 17

When Jesus had spoken these words, he lifted up his eyes to heaven, and said, "Father, the hour has come; glorify your Son that the Son may glorify you, since you have given him authority over all flesh, to give eternal life to all whom you have given him. And this is eternal life, that they know you the only true God, and Jesus Christ whom you have sent. I glorified you on earth, having accomplished the work that you gave me to do. And now, Father, glorify me in your own presence with the glory that I had with you before the world existed.

"I have manifested your name to the people whom you gave me out of the world. Yours they were, and you gave them to me, and they have kept your word. Now they know that everything that you have given me is from you. For I have given them the words that you gave me, and they have received them and have come to know in truth that I came from you; and they have believed that you sent me. I am praying for them. I am not praying for the world but for those whom you have given me, for they are yours. All mine are yours, and yours are mine, and I am glorified in them. And I am no longer in the world, but they are in the world, and I am coming to you. Holy Father, keep them in your name, which you have given me, that they may be one, even as we are one. While I was with them, I kept them in your name, which you have given me. I have guarded them, and not one of them has been lost except the son of destruction, that the Scripture might be fulfilled. But now I am coming to you, and these things I speak in the world, that they may have my joy fulfilled in themselves. I have given them your word, and the world has hated them because they are not of the world, just as I am not of the world. I do not ask that you take them out of the world, but that you keep them from the evil one. They are not of the world, just as I am not of the world. Sanctify them in the truth; your word is truth. As you sent me into the world, so I have sent them into the world. And for their sake I consecrate myself, that they also may be sanctified in truth.

"I do not ask for these only, but also for those who will believe in me through their word, that they may all be one, just as you, Father, are in me, and I in you, that they also may be in us, so that the world may believe that you have sent me. The glory that you have given me I have given to them, that they may be one even as we are one, I in them and you in me, that they may become perfectly one, so that the world may know that you sent me and loved them even as you loved me. Father, I desire that they also, whom you have given me, may be with me where I am, to see my glory that you have given me because you loved me before the foundation of the world. O righteous Father, even though the world does not know you, I know you, and these know that you have sent me. I made known to them your name, and I will continue to make it known, that the love with which you have loved me may be in them, and I in them."

Appendix 4

# A Golden Chain
# by William Perkins
# (1558–1602)

The chart that follows is a redrawing and reframing of one made by the famous Puritan William Perkins. I have augmented it in some areas and have omitted other parts of it.

My desire in offering you this simple diagram is to help you see the ways in which the Lord Jesus's union with us through his incarnation and work brings to us unfathomable blessings. Perhaps you can make a copy of it to carry with you so that when you find yourself faced with the experience of lostness, aloneness, despair, or unbelief, you can look at it.

| *The Work of the Trinity* | *The Work of Faith in Us* | *How These Truths Assure Us* |
|---|---|---|
| God's foreknowledge, decree, predestination, creation, the fall, our state of unbelief | From before creation and the fall of mankind, God the Father had already predestined to save for his glory a people. | Jesus Christ and the salvation we enjoy are not an afterthought or Plan B. It was God's plan from the "beginning" to save sinners and bring them to himself. |
| Jesus Christ is the mediator of the elect | Faith informs that the Lord Jesus stands as Mediator between God the Father against whom we have sinned and our hopeless plight. | We are called by the Father to believe in the Son by the faith granted to us by the Spirit. He had done this so that we can be his forever. |
| The holiness of his manhood | Faith informs us that through the incarnation he is qualified to be our Representative and is therefore authorized to impute righteousness to us. | We can fight against our doubt by remembering that he took human flesh to himself so that he could represent us perfectly. If he would do this for us, we do not need to worry that he will abandon us in our times of temptation and trial. |
| He fulfills the law | He brings us faith to believe that in every way we fail to obey the inviolable law of God and would therefore be subject to God's wrath and curse, he has already gone before us, obeyed the law in our place and has earned the right to grant or impute to us his righteousness. | We can shun despair and draw near to God because the Father no longer looks at us at his enemy, but rather as a beloved child. |
| His accursed death | By dying in our place, the Spirit grants us faith to believe that he has paid for all our sins; that when God looks at us our record is "just as if we had never sinned." Through this knowledge the enslaving power of sin in our lives is broken. | By remembering his accursed death we can be assured that we are completely cleansed from sin and welcomed by the Father. In this we are given faith to war against the sin that so "easily besets" and to know that we are simultaneously justified and sinner. |
| His burial | By faith we believe that in his manhood he actually died in our place, making him our perfect Representative-Brother. He didn't merely black out. This means that our record of debt for sin has been completely paid. Being freed from guilt and the law's punishing demands, the power of sin, which is the law and our failure to obey it, has been broken in our lives. | In light of his death and burial, we can pursue holiness knowing that our standing before the Father is not based upon our performance. By his physical death we are assured that we are completely and eternally one with him, so we can fight against sin in faith. We are also freed from the fear of the isolation of the grave, knowing that he will be with us there, too. |
| His bondage under the grave | Knowing that he suffered our death for us reminds us of our forgiveness, thereby breaking the power of sin in our lives. He was held in death's cold grip for three days so that the eternal price of death for sin would be paid. | We are no longer burdened by the fear of the curse of death for sin, first visited upon Adam and then upon his entire race. The curse of death for sin has been obliterated by Jesus. |

| The Work of the Trinity | The Work of Faith in Us | How These Truths Assure Us |
| --- | --- | --- |
| His resurrection | By the resurrection we can know that the work Jesus did as our Representative was completely sufficient and accepted by the Father in payment for our sins. We can also be assured that the perfectly obedient life produced enough righteousness to cover us all. | Through Jesus's vindication in the resurrection, we are vindicated. Freed from doubt about God's disposition to us or his Son's work, we can know that all he set out to do, to "seek and save the lost," he has accomplished. Through this good news, we have been granted a new life and have faith to repent of our unbelief and sin. Death no longer has a hold on us. Though we do die physically, the spiritual death that was the just wage for our sin has been eliminated. |
| His ascension | In receiving Jesus, the God-man back into heaven, still incarnate, humankind was welcomed back into the presence of God, for he has taken our flesh into the very throne room of heaven. | We have faith to believe that God has accepted as his children all those who believe that the man Jesus is also the Son whom the Father sent to fulfill his will. Jesus is welcomed home, so will we be for he is there, preparing a place for us. |
| He is seated at the right hand of God | Not only was Jesus welcomed back into heaven as a man, but he was also welcomed as King who would rule over all creation. | We have faith to believe that we are not alone; our Brother is, in fact, the man who is ruling and overruling right now from heaven for our good. He is not powerless to comfort and sustain us, nor does anything come into our lives without his express consent. |
| He is interceding for us | Rather than sitting back and waiting for things to wrap up here and for us to get our collective acts together, like the good Husband he is, Jesus is presently praying for us, his bride, that our faith will not fail. | No matter what comes into our lives today, we can persevere in faith believing that he loves us, is praying for us, and will not allow anything into our lives that will destroy our faith. |
| His return | Rather than hiding in heaven like a defeated King, our Lord is waiting for the day when, according to the Father's plan, he will return to claim his rightful earthly kingdom, establish a new heaven and a new earth where righteousness will dwell. | While we await his second advent we can live in hope knowing that the circumstances of our lives here is not all there is. A glorious future of peace and joy await us where all that has been bent and destroyed will be set right, and we will live eternally in the light of his glorious countenance. |
| All to God's glory | All that the Lord Jesus did from the covenant of redemption, through his incarnation, sinless life, substitutionary death, bodily resurrection, ascension, reign and return is for the ultimate glory of God the Father. | Seeing ourselves as being one with him, his being one with us, and our being found in him will, first of all, comfort us in knowing that we will never be without him and, secondly, will spur us on to good works all for God's glory. |

# Notes

*Introduction*

1. Thomas F. Torrance, *Incarnation: The Person and Life of Christ* (Downers Grove, IL: IVP Academic, 2008), 62.
2. Martin Chemnitz, *The Two Natures in Christ*, trans. J. A. O. Preus (St. Louis, MO: Concordia, 1971), 41.
3. John Murray, *Redemption Accomplished and Applied* (Grand Rapids, MI: Eerdmans, 1955), 161.
4. Torrance, *Incarnation*, 20, emphasis added.
5. Charles Wesley, "And Can It Be That I Should Gain?," 1738.

*Chapter 1: From Beginning to End It's All about Him*

1. Dennis E. Johnson, *Him We Proclaim: Preaching Christ from All the Scriptures* (Phillipsburg, NJ: P&R, 2007), 17.
2. If this is a new thought for you, please see John 1:45; 8:56; Acts 26:22; 28:23; Heb. 11:26; 1 Pet. 1:10–12; Jude 5. Jesus is the primary figure of the Old Testament, and every writer of the New Testament attests to it.
3. Moses, the Prophets, and the Psalms were the three categories into which all the Old Testament was divided. When Jesus refers to these three categories, he means every part of the Old Testament, not just the Decalogue, Prophetic Books, or the Psalms.
4. "The covenant of redemption is a mutual compact between the Father and the Son in reference to the salvation of man. This is a subject which, from its nature, is entirely beyond our comprehension. . . . The covenant between the Father and the Son was formed in eternity and revealed in time. . . . Christ speaks of promises made to Him before His advent and of His coming into the world in execution of a commission which He had received from the Father. . . . As Adam was the head and representative of his posterity, so Christ is the head and representative of His people. And as God entered into covenant with Adam, so He entered into covenant with Christ. This, in Romans 5:12–21, is set forth as the fundamental idea of all God's dealings with men, both in their fall and in their redemption." Charles Hodge, *Systematic Theology*, abridged ed., ed. Edward N. Gross (Phillipsburg, NJ: P&R, 1992), 340.
5. Thomas F. Torrance, Robert T. Walker, editors, *Incarnation: The Person and Life of Christ* (Downers Grove, IL: IVP Academic, 2008), 38.
6. See also Ps. 2:7 with Acts 13:33; Mic. 5:2.
7. The phrase "finger of God" is used to speak of God's direct intervention in creation, intervention that was accomplished by the Son. Jesus also used this phrase to speak of himself and his power over Satan.
8. See Rom. 5:9.
9. Torrance, *Incarnation*, 2.

*Chapter 2: Come Adore on Bended Knee*

1. Martin Chemnitz, a follower of Martin Luther, described the incarnation in this way: "The Son of God in the fullness of time joined to Himself in a perpetual union which shall not be dissolved for all eternity, a human nature, true, completely, entire, of the same substance of ours, possessing a body and a rational soul which contain within themselves all the conditions, desires, powers, and faculties proper to and characteristic of human nature. This nature is pure, without sin, incorrupt and holy, yet in it are all the infirmities which have befallen our nature as the penalties of sin. This he willingly and without imperfection assumed at the time of His humiliation, for our sakes, that He might be made the victim for

us." Martin Chemnitz, *The Two Natures in Christ*, trans. J. A. O. Preus (St Louis, MO: Concordia, 1971), 64–65, emphasis added.

2. Wayne Grudem, *Systematic Theology: An Introduction to Biblical Doctrine* (Grand Rapids, MI: Zondervan, 1994), 529.

3. Chemnitz, *Two Natures*, 41.

4. Grudem, *Systematic Theology*, 534.

5. Charles Hodge, *Systematic Theology*, abridged ed., ed. Edward N. Gross (Phillipsburg, NJ: P&R, 1992), 363.

6. Charles Wesley, "Hark! The Herald Angels Sing," 1739.

7. "The thought is present, however, that the conception of Jesus was due to the action of the Holy Spirit. The language is reminiscent of the creation account in Genesis 1, where the Spirit (or wind) of God hovered over the primeval waters. The birth of Jesus thus marks a new creation, a new beginning, equally due to the creative energies of God." Robert Letham, *The Work of Christ*, Contours of Christian Theology, ed. Gerald Bray (Downers Grove, IL: InterVarsity, 1993), 79.

8. Rod Rosenblatt, from unpublished class notes on Martin Chemnitz's *The Two Natures in Christ*, available at Faith Lutheran Church, Capistrano Beach.

9. The name yᵉhôšua, transliterated "Jesus," means "Yahweh will save."

10. Louis Berkhof, *Systematic Theology*, new combined ed. (Grand Rapids, MI: Eerdmans, 1996), 620.

11. Hodge, *Systematic Theology*, 341.

12. Wayne Grudem, *Bible Doctrine: Essential Teachings of the Christian Faith* (Grand Rapids, MI: Zondervan, 1999), 230.

13. Thomas F. Torrance, *Incarnation: The Person and Life of Christ*, ed. Robert T. Walker (Downers Grove, IL: IVP Academic, 2008), 106.

14. Ibid., 64.

15. Martin Luther, "From Heaven Above to Earth I Come," 1535.

*Chapter 3: Our Perfected Savior*

1. John Murray, *Redemption Accomplished and Applied* (Grand Rapids, MI: Eerdmans, 1955), 23–24.

2. *ESV Study Bible*, ed. Wayne Grudem (Wheaton, IL: Crossway, 2008), note on John 1:23.

3. Robert Letham, *Union with Christ: In Scripture, History, and Theology*, (Phillipsburg, NJ: P&R, 2011), 138.

4. Martin Chemnitz, *The Two Natures in Christ*, trans. J. A. O. Preus (St. Louis, MO: Concordia, 1972), 62.

5. Thomas F. Torrance, *Incarnation: The Person and Life of Christ* (Downers Grove, IL: IVP Academic, 2008), 147.

6. Letham, *Union with Christ*, 79.

*Chapter 4: God's Love for Sinners*

1. Martin Chemnitz, *The Two Natures in Christ*, trans. J. A. O. Preus (St. Louis, MO: Concordia, 1971), 357.

2. E. E. Carpenter and P. W. Comfort, *Holman Treasury of Key Bible Words: 200 Greek and 200 Hebrew Words Defined and Explained* (Nashville, TN: Broadman, 2000), 407.

3. C. H. Spurgeon, *The Gospel of the Kingdom: A Commentary on the Book of Matthew* (London: Passmore and Alabaster, 1893), 141.

4. J. E. Smith, *The Books of History*. Old Testament Survey (Joplin, MO: College Press, 1995), n.p.

5. "Jesus would not let the demons say who he was (Mark 1:34; 3:12; Luke 4:41); see that you tell no one (Matt. 8:4); he charged the leper not to tell anyone (Mark 1:44; Luke 5:14); also the blind men (Matt. 9:30); he gave strict orders that no one should know of [the miracles] (Mark 5:43); do not even enter the village (Mark 8:26); he told them to tell no one what had happened (Luke 8:56); Jesus warned them not to make him known (Matt. 12:16); he charged them to tell no one (Mark 7:36); he warned his disciples not to say he was the Christ (Matt. 16:20; Mark 8:30; Luke 9:21); not to tell anyone about the transfiguration (Matt. 17:9; Mark 9:9), which they did not (Luke 9:36); Jesus did not want anyone to know he was in a house (Mark 7:24); he would not have anyone know he was in Galilee (Mark 9:30); neither will I tell you by what authority I do these things (Matt. 21:27; Mark 11:33; Luke 20:8)." C. A. Day, *Collins Thesaurus of the Bible* (Bellingham, WA: Logos Research Systems, 2009).

6. A. T. Robertson, *Word Pictures in the New Testament* (Nashville, TN: Broadman, 1933), n.p.

*Notes*

Chapter 5: *O Sacred Head, Now Wounded*
1. Girolamo Savonarola, "Jesus, Refuge of the Weary," 1563.

Chapter 6: *Jesus Shall Reign*
1. F. W. Krummacher, *The Risen Redeemer: The Gospel History from the Resurrection to the Day of Pentecost*, trans. John T. Betts (London: James Nisbet, 1862), 7.
2. By the way, angels don't look like blond women with wings. If you ever saw an angel, you would be terrified, much as the guards were who trembled and fainted. You certainly wouldn't ask one to sit atop your Christmas tree.
3. Though scholars are not in complete agreement on the number, one can identify at least nine appearances of Christ after his resurrection, gathered from the following texts: Matt. 28:9, 17; Mark 16:9; Luke 24:15, 36, 50; John 20:19, 26; 21:1; Acts 1:1–8; 9:5. Kenneth O. Gangel, *John*, Holman New Testament Commentary, ed. Max Anders (Nashville, TN: Broadman, 2000), 394.
4. Don't misunderstand: the only difference between Peter and Judas was that Jesus had prayed for Peter that his faith would not fail (Luke 22:32), so he had been granted repentance. On the morning of the resurrection, Peter had run to the tomb and seen that it was empty, but he didn't have any conversation with the friend he had deserted. We know that the Lord had appeared to him one other time (Luke 24:34), but we're not given any details about a conversation between them.
5. Gerrit Scott Dawson, *Jesus Ascended: The Meaning of Christ's Continuing Incarnation* (Phillipsburg, NJ: P&R, 2004), 111.
6. Robert Letham, *Union with Christ: In Scripture, History, and Theology* (Phillipsburg, NJ: P&R, 2011), 41.
7. Isaac Watts, "Jesus Shall Reign," 1719.

Introduction to Part 2
1. John Murray, *Redemption Accomplished and Applied* (Grand Rapids, MI: Eerdmans, 1955), 161.

Chapter 7: "*I in Them*"
1. *ESV Study Bible*, ed. Wayne Grudem (Wheaton, IL: Crossway, 2008), note on Rom. 6:4.
2. We will consider this point in greater detail in chapter 10.
3. What follows is a list of all the "in Christ" statements from the Pauline corpus as translated in the ESV. It does not include any "in him" or "in the Lord" verses or any verses from other translations. This list is given primarily so that you might get a sense of how deep and rich the doctrine of our "in-ness" with Christ is. In the book of Romans we have redemption (3:24); we are dead to sin and alive to God (Rom 6:11); we have eternal life (Rom 6:23); we have no condemnation (8:1); we have freedom (8:2); we have the love of God (8:39); we are one body with the church and the Lord (12:5). In 1 Corinthians, in him we are sanctified (1:2); we have grace (1:4); we have wisdom from God, righteousness, sanctification, and redemption (1:30); we've been made alive (15:22). In 2 Corinthians we learn that in Christ we are led in triumphal procession (2:14); we are new creations (5:17); we've been reconciled with God (5:19). In Galatians we have freedom from the law's demands (Gal 2:4); we are justified (2:16); we have inherited all the blessings of Abraham (3:14); we are sons of God (3:26); we have been made one new race (3:28); we are free from the demands of the law for merit before God (5:6). In Ephesians (a book absolutely loaded with union allusions) we have been blessed with every spiritual blessing (1:3); we have been raised up and seated with Christ (2:6); we have been created for good works and enabled to do them (2:10); we have been brought near (2:13); we are partakers of the promise made to Abraham (3:6); we have been given forgiveness (4:32). In Philippians we are found in him (Phil 3:9); and we have every need supplied (4:19). In 1 Thessalonians we are assured of resurrection for the dead (4:16); we are assured that we'll have true and eternal life (2 Tim 1:1). In 2 Timothy we are recipients of grace (1:9); we are recipients of salvation (2:10).
4. John Murray, *Redemption Accomplished and Applied* (Grand Rapids, MI: Eerdmans, 1955), 168.
5. *ESV Study Bible*, notes on Col. 1:26–27.
6. By the way, it is important for women (as well as for men) to think of themselves as "sons" when considering the topic of adoption. That is because a Roman son had rights and privileges that daughters did not have. Sons had rights of inheritance and authority that were not given to women, no matter how beloved they were. Ladies, this is one of those times when we need to think of ourselves as masculine, as "sons," just as the men need to think of themselves as feminine when we talk about being Christ's bride.

7. J. Todd Billings, *Union with Christ: Reframing Theology and Ministry for the Church* (Grand Rapids, MI: Baker Academic, 2011), 21.
8. Ibid.
9. Philip Doddridge, "Dear Saviour, I Am Thine, by Everlasting Bands," in Charles H. Spurgeon, *Our Own Hymn Book: A Collection of Psalms and Hymns for Public, Social, and Private Worship* (London: Passmore and Alabaster, n.d.).

*Chapter 8: He Gave Himself Up for Us*

1. Of course the commands or imperatives have been put there by the Holy Spirit for our instruction and should never be ignored. It is just that my purpose now is to focus on Christ's relationship with the church, his bride, and it is very hard for us to read anything about our work without diminishing his.
2. A. H. Strong, *Systematic Theology* (Philadelphia: American Baptist Publication Society, 1907), 795–96.
3. John Murray, *Redemption Accomplished and Applied* (Grand Rapids, MI: Eerdmans, 1955), 165.
4. See my *Helper by Design: God's Perfect Plan for Women in Marriage* (Chicago: Moody, 2003), 34.
5. Which, of course, is why homosexuality is an insult to the Lord's creation order. When a man (or a woman) loves another of his or her own gender, he or she will never be whole. Male and female need their counterparts to complete them, which is also why even in homosexual couples there is always a masculine and a feminine. Some people are gifted with singleness, and to those people God has granted a wholeness with him that transcends those not so gifted.
6. In his incarnation, the man Christ Jesus demonstrated his need for communion and fellowship with others in many ways, not the least of which was his desire to have his friends with him as he labored in Gethsemane. In his deity, Jesus had all the union he needed, but in his humanity he needed other human beings with whom he could fellowship and ultimately be one.
7. *ESV Study Bible*, ed. Wayne Grudem (Wheaton, IL: Crossway, 2008), note on Eph. 1:23.
8. Ibid., note on 1 Cor. 6:14.
9. F. W. Krummacher, *The Suffering Savior* (1856; repr. Carlisle, PA: Banner of Truth, 2004), 10.

*Chapter 9: Chosen, Betrothed, Beloved, and Named*

1. C. S. Lewis, *That Hideous Strength* (New York: Scribner, 2003), 316.
2. *ESV Study Bible*, ed. Wayne Grudem (Wheaton, IL: Crossway, 2008), note on 1 Thess. 1:4.
3. "On the one hand, God predestines some to be saved. On the other hand, God still longs for all to be saved. . . . Though it may seem impossible to understand how both of these statements are true, the Bible teaches both, and one should not use either truth to deny the other." *ESV Study Bible* note on Rom. 10:20–21.
4. I'm not making any comment here about the cessation or continuance of the gifts of the Spirit as mentioned in 1 Corinthians 12 and Romans 12. In any case, whether you believe the gifts are still extant or not, the truth remains that they were/are Christ's gift to her bride.
5. L. Berkhof, *Systematic Theology* (Grand Rapids, MI: Eerdmans, 1938), 513.
6. Ibid., 517.

*Chapter 10: You Are Forgiven, You Are Righteous, You Are Loved*

1. For more on this topic, please see my *Idols of the Heart: Learning to Long for God Alone* (Phillipsburg, NJ: P&R, 2002).
2. Jerry Bridges, *The Discipline of Grace: God's Role and Our Role in the Pursuit of Holiness* (Colorado Springs, CO: NavPress, 2006), 74.

*Appendix 1: The Creeds*

1. Wayne Grudem, *Systematic Theology* (Grand Rapids, MI: Zondervan, 1995), 530.
2. Both the Mormon and Jehovah's Witnesses have incorrect understandings of the incarnation and the nature and work of Jesus Christ. Although it might not seem like a big deal, faulty belief on this topic can mean the difference between salvation and damnation.

# General Index

Abraham, 33–36
Adam, 31–32, 55, 63, 74, 140, 166–67
adoption, 149–51, 226
angels, 56–57, 115–16, 226
Apollinarius, 208
Apostles' Creed, 209
ascension, 128–30, 168, 223
assurance, 222–23
Athanasian Creed, 210–11
atonement, 35, 38, 161–64, 184

baptism, 66, 138–40
born again, 39, 214
Bridges, Jerry, 201

Caiaphas, 101–2
Calvary, 34–35, 103–8
Chemnitz, Martin, 224–25
circumcision, 49–50
Communion, 36
conflict, 31
Council of Chalcedon, 209
Council of Constantinople, 208
Council of Ephesus, 209
covenants, 49–50, 224
creation, 29–32, 222

Day, C. A., 225
death, 119–20, 127–28, 140–41, 222
disunity, 31
doubt, 125–26, 222
dower, 176–77

election, 174–76
Elijah, 80–83
eternal life, 39, 119, 128, 140–42
Eutyches, 209
Eve, 31–32

faith, 74, 128, 138, 192, 223
fall, 30–32, 222
forgiveness, 185–87, 197–98, 203

Gethsemane, 98–99
God, glory of, 37–38, 84, 223; image of, 31–32, 166; judgment of, 38–39, 142–43; love of, 77–78, 144, 192–93, 198–200; pleasure of, 21–22; promises of blessing, 33–34
gossip, 198
grace, 30, 107, 114, 193, 203

holiness, 61, 222
Holy Spirit, 48, 66–67, 75, 145, 151, 158, 168, 191, 214, 227
homosexuality, 227
Hosea, 178–79
humility, 22–23, 101

idolatry, 196–97
impeccability, 72
Isaac, 34–35
isolation, 17–18, 31–32

229

# Scripture Index

*Scripture Index*

232

| | |
|---|---|
| 27:29 | 103 |
| 27:31 | 103 |
| 27:46 | 35, 104 |
| 27:65–66 | 114 |
| 28:2 | 115 |
| 28:3 | 115 |
| 28:5–6 | 116 |
| 28:6 | 127 |
| 28:8–10 | 117 |
| 28:9 | 226 |
| 28:17 | 226 |

**Mark**

| | |
|---|---|
| 1:13 | 68 |
| 1:22 | 79 |
| 1:34 | 225 |
| 1:44 | 225 |
| 3:12 | 225 |
| 5:43 | 225 |
| 7:24 | 225 |
| 7:36 | 225 |
| 8:26 | 225 |
| 8:30 | 225 |
| 8:31 | 115 |
| 9:9 | 225 |
| 9:30 | 225 |
| 9:31 | 115 |
| 10:34 | 115 |
| 10:45 | 138, 166 |
| 11:33 | 225 |
| 13:32 | 53 |
| 14:7–8 | 86 |
| 14:24 | 166 |
| 14:36 | 100 |
| 15:37 | 108 |
| 15:39 | 108 |
| 15:46 | 109 |
| 16:3 | 115 |
| 16:8 | 116 |
| 16:9 | 226 |

**Luke**

| | |
|---|---|
| 1:32–33 | 56 |
| 1:35 | 48, 50, 56 |
| 1:51–53 | 115 |
| 2:10–11 | 56 |

| | |
|---|---|
| 2:14 | 56, 92 |
| 2:20 | 57 |
| 2:40 | 51 |
| 2:47 | 53 |
| 2:51 | 54 |
| 2:52 | 55 |
| 3:21 | 65 |
| 3:23–38 | 50 |
| 4:5 | 70 |
| 4:17–19 | 73 |
| 4:21 | 73 |
| 4:41 | 225 |
| 5:14 | 225 |
| 7 | 92 |
| 8:56 | 225 |
| 9:21 | 225 |
| 9:22 | 84 |
| 9:23–25 | 198–99 |
| 9:28–36 | 80 |
| 9:35 | 81 |
| 9:36 | 225 |
| 9:44 | 85 |
| 10:27 | 60 |
| 19:10 | 181 |
| 20:8 | 225 |
| 22:32 | 226 |
| 22:33 | 97 |
| 22:44 | 99 |
| 22:45 | 99 |
| 23:34 | 104 |
| 23:43 | 104 |
| 23:46 | 108 |
| 24:5 | 116 |
| 24:11 | 117 |
| 24:13–27 | 122 |
| 24:15 | 226 |
| 24:25–26 | 122 |
| 24:27 | 27, 29, 81 |
| 24:30–31 | 122 |
| 24:32 | 81 |
| 24:34 | 122, 226 |
| 24:36 | 226 |
| 24:36–43 | 125 |
| 24:44 | 29 |
| 24:50 | 226 |

| | |
|---|---|
| 3:25 | 33 |
| 4:11 | 145 |
| 4:24–28 | 109 |
| 7:37 | 36 |
| 9:3–5 | 126 |
| 9:5 | 226 |
| 10:39–40 | 125 |
| 13:33 | 224 |
| 15:14–18 | 182 |
| 26:22 | 224 |
| 28:23 | 224 |

**Romans**

| | |
|---|---|
| 1:7 | 174 |
| 3:23 | 216 |
| 3:23–25 | 137 |
| 3:24 | 226 |
| 3:26 | 163 |
| 4:7–8 | 184 |
| 4:25 | 98 |
| 5:6–8 | 216 |
| 5:9 | 224 |
| 5:12–21 | 224 |
| 5:18–19 | 186 |
| 5:19 | 74 |
| 6 | 142 |
| 6:3–4 | 138 |
| 6:4 | 226 |
| 6:11 | 138, 226 |
| 6:21 | 140 |
| 6:23 | 140, 216, 226 |
| 7 | 142 |
| 7:4 | 159 |
| 7:5 | 139 |
| 7:15 | 142 |
| 7:18–19 | 142 |
| 7:24 | 142 |
| 7:25 | 142 |
| 8:1 | 142, 217, 226 |
| 8:2 | 143, 226 |
| 8:3–4 | 142–43 |
| 8:4 | 186 |
| 8:10–11 | 148 |
| 8:15–17 | 150 |
| 8:21 | 195 |
| 8:35 | 13 |

| | |
|---|---|
| 8:35–36 | 170 |
| 8:38–39 | 160, 170 |
| 8:39 | 226 |
| 9:25–26 | 178 |
| 10:9–13 | 216 |
| 10:12 | 177 |
| 10:20–21 | 227 |
| 11:36 | 177 |
| 12 | 227 |
| 12:5 | 226 |
| 16:20 | 33 |

**1 Corinthians**

| | |
|---|---|
| 1:2 | 226 |
| 1:4 | 226 |
| 1:26 | 47 |
| 1:30 | 183, 226 |
| 3:16 | 145 |
| 3:22–23 | 150 |
| 6:11 | 183 |
| 6:14 | 227 |
| 6:15 | 167 |
| 6:17 | 22, 159 |
| 7:39 | 161 |
| 10:3–4 | 36 |
| 10:9 | 70 |
| 12 | 177, 227 |
| 12:12 | 155, 167 |
| 12:27 | 22, 167 |
| 15:1–8 | 121 |
| 15:14 | 126 |
| 15:17 | 113, 121, 128 |
| 15:20 | 120 |
| 15:22 | 226 |
| 15:23 | 120 |
| 15:45 | 143 |
| 15:49 | 22 |

**2 Corinthians**

| | |
|---|---|
| 2:14 | 226 |
| 4:6 | 23 |
| 5:17 | 217, 226 |
| 5:18–19 | 166 |
| 5:19 | 226 |
| 5:21 | 35, 74, 98, 216 |
| 6:14 | 161 |

# Study *Found in Him* with a Group!

## Companion Workbook and Teaching DVD are
### Now Available at ElyseFitzpatrick.com

Follow along with Elyse Fitzpatrick on her teaching DVD* as she explores the wonder of the incarnation and the glory of the Christian's unbreakable connection to Christ.

Each DVD session gives an overview of one chapter in the book. A workbook is also available for women who would like to follow along the DVD with the teaching outline. Discussion questions for group settings can be found at the end of each book chapter.

*The DVDs include 10 sessions, each corresponding to a chapter in the book. Each session is approximately 20 minutes in length.*

# Also Available from Elyse Fitzpatrick

GIVE THEM
*grace*

*Dazzling Your Kids
with the Love of Jesus*

Elyse M. Fitzpatrick & Jessica Thompson

connecting
broken people
to the love
of Christ

COUNSEL FROM THE CROSS

Elyse M. Fitzpatrick and
Dennis E. Johnson

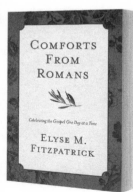

COMFORTS
FROM
ROMANS

*Celebrating the Gospel One Day at a Time*

ELYSE M.
FITZPATRICK

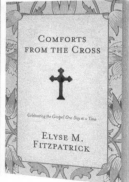

COMFORTS
FROM THE CROSS

*Celebrating the Gospel One Day at a Time*

ELYSE M.
FITZPATRICK

BECAUSE HE
LOVES ME

*How Christ Transforms Our Daily Life*

ELYSE M.
FITZPATRICK